leetwood Mac

the Complete uide *to their* Music

PRESS
w York
penhagen
d/Tokyo

Rikky Rooksby

Contents

INTRODUCTION

FEW BANDS HAVE SUCH A REMARKABLE HISTORY AS FLEETWOOD MAC. International stardom is something that only a handful of groups ever attain. Fleetwood Mac achieved it not once but *twice*, with two different line-ups and two contrasting styles of music. As a result, Fleetwood Mac almost has two audiences. For some people the band's name conjures up late Sixties British blues, 'Albatross' or 'Man Of The World'. For others, Fleetwood Mac is Californian FM rock, 'Rhiannon' or 'Don't Stop' or 'Little Lies'. Some think they're English, some think they're American. Some think they split in 1970, others that they started in 1975. It's a confusing picture. Many line-up changes mean that tracing the history of the Mac - who recorded what, when and with whom - can be bewildering. Their recorded legacy is contained on no less than 20 studio albums, a number of greatest hits collections, a variety of live recordings, and a pile of compilations. And that's where this book comes in, as a tour guide to the epic trials, tantrums and tribulations of the band ... no, let's call it the saga .. of Fleetwood Mac.

The origins of Fleetwood Mac lie in the blues boom of mid-Sixties London. Guitarist Peter Green teamed up with Mick Fleetwood (drums), John McVie (bass) and Jeremy Spencer (guitar) to form a group steeped in a desire to faithfully recreate electric blues. Green had just come from a stint with John Mayall's Bluesbreakers, having had the unenviable task of filling Eric Clapton's shoes after he departed to form Cream. On the LP *A Hard Road*, Green rose to the challenge, demonstrating considerable taste and that he had an authentic guitar voice of his own. Green was so enamoured of his new rhythm section that he made up the band's name from a combination of theirs - Fleetwood and Mac from 'McVie'. In Jeremy Spencer the band found a dyed-in-the-wool blues obsessive who had perfected an Elmore James-slide guitar style. Armed with this twin guitar front and the contrasting vocal styles of Green and Spencer, Fleetwood Mac cut their first album and headed off to the club circuit. This was the age of heavy, and not so heavy, blues. Even the folk guitarists (see Pentangle) were playing adaptations of the 12-bar.

As might have been guessed from the reticent poetry of his lead guitar, Green was said to be uncomfortable with the spotlight being on him so much. A third guitarist joined the band, fresh-faced Danny Kirwan, giving the Mac a new resource but heightening tensions within the band's creative make-up. Kirwan brought something of a pop sensibility to the proceedings, some of his songs sounding like a watered-down version of West Coast rock. Fleetwood Mac now discovered they were in danger of going in too many directions at once. They had pop material, blues covers, blues originals, and Spencer's penchant for '50s rock'n'roll pastiche, which led him to write songs like 'Buddy's Song', full of hiccupping references to the late bespectacled singer. And then there was Green's own genius for poignant minor key blues instrumentals and groundbreaking numbers like 'Oh Well' and 'Albatross'. The inner divisions didn't affect the record sales, and it was rumoured that in 1969 the band were outselling the Beatles. Unlike Led Zeppelin, the other huge band of that year, the Mac were not averse to releasing singles that climbed to the top of the UK charts.

The end came quickly and unpredictably. At the height of their success, Peter Green decided to quit the music business. This was the result of a number of factors. He had been the victim of a malign drug experience. He was tormented by his conscience because of the large amounts of money the band were earning, feeling that it should go to charity. He was also feeling musically frustrated. Apart from a couple of solo albums, that was the last that was heard of him for two decades. Spencer and Kirwan tried to carry on, but a short while later Spencer quit to join a religious group called the Children of God. The first Fleetwood Mac was over.

McVie and Fleetwood struggled on with a number of line-ups and eventually re-located to the US. The most important new recruit was Christine Perfect, the partner of McVie, who became a vocalist and keyboard player, but Bob Welch was a stalwart member during these hard years. During the early Seventies the band cut half a dozen indifferent albums enlivened only by the occasional good song. This was Mac's waste-land period. It signalled an important change of musical direction away from the band's blues roots to a mainstream rock sound, but the real turning point came in 1974 when the band joined up with the American duo of Stevie Nicks and Lindsey Buckingham. The first album they cut became a massive success on the back of a gruelling tour schedule and several hit singles. Its follow-up was the mega-platinum *Rumours*, which became one of the biggest-selling albums in the history of rock. Fleetwood Mac had become a huge-selling act for the second time, a feat almost unparalleled.

Why did it happen then? The mid-Seventies Fleetwood Mac played music guaranteed to find a large audience. They looked good. The music was easy-listening rock-a-steady rolling rhythm, contrasting male and female voices, block harmonies in the best West Coast tradition, acoustic and electric guitars, the occasional lead solo for the boys, a touch of electric piano, short songs with radio-friendly hooks. Stevie Nicks added a little sparkle of ballet-shoed, permed mystique on songs like 'Rhiannon'. They wrote about love, and in particular – on *Rumours* - they wrote about the relationships within the band but did it in a way that was easy on the ear. The audience became voyeurs, watching the best soap opera in rock, guessing from the couplings and uncouplings on the album covers (and the cover of *Rolling Stone*) who was going out with whom (and feeling sorry for the towering Mick Fleetwood, who always seemed to get left out). This audience could also relate its own romantic troubles to the same music. And from the archaeological angle Fleetwood Mac were a band with a skeleton in its closet (what had happened to all those earlier guitarists?), like a dance around a cenotaph to the lost warriors of the Sixties rock wars.

With *Rumours*, Fleetwood Mac went ballistic. If JFK were still President he would probably have ordered a naval blockade of them. Of course, that kind of success cannot last. You can't be that far up without bumping your head on the Van Allen belt and giving your accountants altitude sickness. The Mac were no exception. But through the Eighties and Nineties, despite more line-up changes, the departure of Nicks and Buckingham, and the fact that the albums came further apart, the Mac retained their popularity and became an institution. Rather like the burger, in fact. With the Mac you always know what you're getting. It's a tape you can put on at parties without offending the clientele. Their position in American culture was fixed by their appearance at Bill Clinton's inauguration. And if you don't like the latest album, there's always that wonderful after-dinner chestnut: which is better - 'Green Manalishi' or 'Tusk', *Then Play On* or *Rumours*, the Buckingham Palace or the Green God? The choice is yours.

In this guide you'll find chapters on all of the original Fleetwood Mac albums in chronological order, including the greatest hits because these collect tracks otherwise not released on studio albums. Compilations, live albums and videos receive separate sections. The compilation area is the trickiest for purchasers simply because the Peter Green period has been subject to considerable re-packaging.

Note to the Revised Edition, 2004

AND THEN PLAY ON. IN THE 1997 EDITION OF THIS BOOK I WROTE THAT FOR FANS of Fleetwood Mac, we were then living in the best of times. The rumours and hopes were fulfilled in the intervening years since I wrote this book. Peter Green not only returned to live performance with the Splinter Group, he recorded several albums of blues material, all of Robert Johnson's repertoire (recently packaged as a 3-CD set *Me And The Devil*), and a live DVD. Jeremy Spencer has also been playing a few gigs; Danny Kirwan has granted the odd interview to guitar magazines. The Green-era band's back-catalogue has turned into a mini-industry of its own, with a bewildering number of new releases.

Fleetwood Mac were inducted into the Rock'n'Roll Hall of Fame in 1998. Four-fifths of the classic Rumours line-up of the Mac have written and recorded a new album, *Say You Will*, and have been tramping across the world playing these and older songs to sell-out audiences. This new album was released in DVD-A as a multi-channel recording, and it is probable that older Mac material will eventually be released in the same format. There have also been indications of a critical re-assessment of the *Tusk* album. Meanwhile, *Rumours* has notched up sales of 19 million and still rising, making it reputedly the sixth best-selling album of all time.

There have been two new Greatest Hits packages. At the time of writing, in the spring of 2004, no less than nine Fleetwood Mac albums are about to be repackaged with extra tracks. Blue Horizon are doing the first six by the Sixties outfit. The later band's trio of sales-breaking albums *Fleetwood Mac*, *Rumours* and *Tusk* will get the archival treatment with bonus CDs of working versions and alternate takes – up to 18 extra tracks to a disc.

My thanks to Martin Willbery and John and Stephanie for loan of materials. I would like to thank Peter Green for giving of his time for an interview in February 1997. The Mick Fleetwood/Stephen Davis biography *Fleetwood*, Mick Fleetwood's illustrated *My Twenty-Five Years In Fleetwood Mac*, and back issues of *Record Collector*, *Music Collector*, and *Guitar* (UK) were useful for checking facts and for some comments by Peter Green. Bill DeMain's interviews of the band in May 2003 in the *Performing Songwriter Magazine* are worth checking out.

The Mac bookshelf has been enhanced by Dinky Dawson's *Life On The Road* (Billboard books), Bob Brunning's *Fleetwood Mac Behind The Masks* (NEL, 1990) reprinted as *The First Thirty Years*, Martin Celmins' *Peter Green: Founder Of Fleetwood Mac* (Sanctuary, rev.ed.1998), and Mick Fleetwood's own *Two Sticks And A Drum* (2002) – the last also available as a DVD. There is also *Fleetwood Mac The Unauthorized Biography* (Chrome Dreams 2003), a CD-audio biography with booklet.

There are quite a few websites devoted to Fleetwood Mac. Try:
www.fleetwoodmac.com
www.petergreen-splintergroup.co.uk
www.jeremyspencer.com
www.frnlegacy.com
www.fleetwoodmac.net

Rikky Rooksby

Peter Green's Fleetwood Mac

US Epic BN 26402 June 1968; UK Blue Horizon 7-63200 February 1968;
reissues UK CBS Embassy EMB 31036 (1973); CBS 31499 (1977);
UK Impact /Line lmlp 4-00216 (Import) white vinyl 1990

THE MUSICIANS WHO ASSEMBLED AS FLEETWOOD MAC IN **1967** HAD BEEN part of the London music scene since the early Sixties. Mick Fleetwood played drums with an outfit called The Cheynes from 1963-65. John McVie played bass for John Mayall from 1963. Peter Green had started off playing bass with Bobby Dennis & The Dominoes, The Muskrats and West London dance band The Tridents. In 1966 Green met up with Fleetwood in the short-lived Shotgun Express, an outfit that also included Rod Stewart, such was the absurd wealth of talented performers in mid-Sixties London. When Shotgun Express split in February 1967, Stewart joined The Jeff Beck Group and Mick Fleetwood became one of The Bluesbreakers.

Peter Green had been drafted into The Bluesbreakers for their *A Hard Road* album when Eric Clapton left in mid-1966. On Green's birthday, Mayall gave the guitarist some free studio time. Green, McVie and Fleetwood used this time to record five tracks: 'Double Trouble', 'It Hurts Me Too' and three instrumentals – 'Curly', 'Rubber Duck' and 'Fleetwood Mac', so-called after the rhythm section (the origin of the band's name). Mick Fleetwood spent about five weeks with The Bluesbreakers in 1967 before getting sacked for excessive drinking. Fleetwood later said: "I didn't have a drink problem when I joined John Mayall, but I may have had one by the time I was fired. I was very sad to leave The Bluesbreakers. I loved playing with McVie, whose style perfectly complemented my own."

Green left not long after and formed the first Fleetwood Mac in the summer of 1967. He wanted bassist John McVie too, but McVie stayed with Mayall because he felt it was more secure, commenting: "I didn't want to join Peter's band because I had a good living and some security. I was making £40 a week and felt I was doing well. But Peter kept tugging at me all that fall, telling me I had to join Fleetwood Mac." The line-up was completed by Jeremy Spencer, whom Mike Vernon (the band's producer) had seen in Birmingham playing with a group called The Levi Set. When Green heard a tape of Spencer's blues guitar he was determined to have him in the band. Even at this early stage, Green loathed the idea of the 'Guitar Hero' and wanted to make sure he didn't get all the attention.

Fleetwood Mac débuted at the Windsor Blues and Jazz Festival on August 12, 1967, with Bob Brunning, who had been recruited through an ad in the *Melody Maker*, on bass. The band played two sets and went down very well. Coincidentally, John McVie was there to see them, and a band called Chicken Shack were also on the bill. They featured an attractive keyboard player called Christine Perfect who would later play a very significant role in the history of Fleetwood Mac.

The band's début single, 'I Believe My Time Ain't Long', was released in October 1967, followed in March 1968 by another non-album track, 'Black Magic Woman', which was in turn followed by a cover of 'Need Your Love So Bad'. By this time a change in Mayall's musical direction made McVie decide it was time to quit The Bluesbreakers for Mac, replacing Bob Brunning who became a school teacher.

Fleetwood Mac's first album stayed in the charts for nine months, such was the interest in this type of white-boy blues in 1968. It was the height of the British blues boom, with bands and performers like Cream, Led Zeppelin, John Mayall and, of course, Jimi Hendrix exploring blues, blooze, rock, psychedelia and improvisation. Producer Mike Vernon recalled the sessions for *Peter Green's Fleetwood Mac* as having "an air of excitement and an expectancy and thankfully never one of feeling under any pressure. Everyone did what they felt as and when they felt it." The intention was to present the band "as they sounded live", so overdubs were minimal. It was recorded in three days on four-track at CBS's New Bond Street studios, which were to be important in the development of the band's use of reverb. *Melody Maker* called it "the best English blues LP ever released here".

Compared with the subsequent début albums by Free and Led Zeppelin, or the Beck/Stewart *Truth* album, much of the material sounds a bit tame, lacking in dynamics and arrangement. The quality also suffered whenever Jeremy Spencer got to the mike. The best tracks are those that feature Peter Green, whose performance throughout is tastefully understated. 'I Loved Another Woman' was a taste of future brilliance from that quarter.

Fleetwood Mac started their long musical journey as a British blues band with just a hint that they might have someone on board whose finesse would make them legendary.

MY HEART BEATS LIKE A HAMMER
(J. Spencer)

THE ALBUM opens with a straight 12-bar in E, Green on the left channel playing rhythm, and Spencer stepping out for the first time with the slide riff borrowed from Elmore James' 'Dust My Broom'. The overall effect is a light boogie feel. The lyric is fairly clichéd and the vocal somewhat mannered, the general aim being to produce an earthy sound.

MERRY GO ROUND
(P.A. Green)

A STEREO drum mix immediately makes this sound spacier. It's another 12-bar with some mildly jazzy semi-tone shifts and some typically reticent guitar fills by Green whose guitar is recorded fairly dry, and without effects. Lyrically, it's another song on the subject the blues seems incapable of exhausting – women – this time of the 'my woman dun me right' variety, rather than 'dun me wrong'. There is no second guitar playing chords, so when Green takes a solo in the middle the whole sound becomes quite empty. The rhythm guitar uses ninth chords dropped in like liquid splashes and there are no great dynamic shifts of volume, only off-mike talking and cries in the best blues tradition.

LONG GREY MARE
(P.A. Green)

A SLIGHTLY quicker equestrian 12-bar using a bass/guitar unison ascending riff and lyrically recycling the old lyric chestnut about ponies/horses/riding etc. There's a harmonica break in the middle and sundry harmonica phrases throughout the verses. The Mac play this with reasonable finesse, sitting straight in the saddle. This was probably one of the four tracks they demoed at Decca's studios with Bob Brunning on bass.

HELLHOUND ON MY TRAIL
(Trad arr. P.A. Green)

F ROM THE horses to the dogs. This is the seminal Robert Johnson song, a six-bar blues sung to a piano accompaniment. There's a brief piano solo in the middle. The dry production on the vocal apes the primitive recording sound of the original blues masters. This fades away quite quickly.

SHAKE YOUR MONEYMAKER
(E. James)

H ERE, FOR the first time, the Mac show an exciting sense of dynamics with the alternating rhythm guitar and the slide with bass and drums, driving along at a faster pace than anything else on the LP so far. Spencer provides slide guitar, an uninspired lead vocal and a guitar solo in the middle, while Green plays clean rhythm in the background. There's a frenetic coda with the band driving as hard as they can to the abrupt conclusion. This found a place on the 1971 *Greatest Hits*, and deservedly so.

LOOKING FOR SOMEBODY
(P.A. Green)

A NOTHER 12-bar with some effectively 'vocal' harmonica on the intro. Green takes the lead vocal over an implied backing in G minor, although for the verse it is only a vocal over a bass riff and drums. There are a few hints of the imaginative approach to arrangement which would enable Green's Fleetwood Mac to create some of their finest tracks. After the harmonica solo the track fades away.

NO PLACE TO GO
(C. Burnett)

A COVER of Howlin' Wolf with his trademark "how many more times" lyric. Green does a passable job on the vocal and supplies the harmonica while playing the single chord E riff throughout with occasional variations. 'No Place To Go' manages to build a reasonable intensity for a first album.

MY BABY'S GOOD TO ME
(J. Spencer)

THIS HAS a slightly denser sound, complete with a doubled rhythm guitar part on the left, and slide fills. Spencer takes the vocal and provides the slide solo in the middle but spends most of the song looking for a melody and lyrics. This sounds rather amateurish now, even if it didn't in 1968. But at least it doesn't make it through the three-minute barrier.

I LOVED ANOTHER WOMAN
(P.A. Green)

WITH quite a shock we hear Green step forward, with his voice and guitar swathed in deep reverb, for this D minor 12-bar. It's very minimal – drums, bass and a single guitar part which counterpoints the melody. Lyrically, it's a song about male infidelity and a bleak recognition of its emotional cost. At the end Green supplies some falsetto vocals which sound like a gentler Howlin' Wolf. Taut, understated and expressive, 'I Loved Another Woman' is one of the stand-out tracks on the album. Its use of reverb points the way to the production on Fleetwood Mac's greatest Sixties recordings.

COLD BLACK NIGHT
(J. Spencer)

WITH A sleight-of-hand intro, we find ourselves in a slow major key blues cruelly exposed by the previous track, as Spencer gets another chance to go looking for that melody he still can't quite find. His slide phrases soon become tiresomely repetitious across the album, though not quite as much as his vocal mannerisms. This is turgid and uninspired. Mercifully it gets faded before too long.

THE WORLD KEEPS ON TURNING
(P.A. Green)

THIS FEATURES Green on acoustic guitar for the first time, in a melancholy one-chord E blues. Some of these guitar figures would eventually be recycled for 'Oh Well'. Occasionally, Green abandons strict time on some of the runs, which gives it a fairly authentic blues feel. The lyrics nod towards the erotic without resulting in exaggeration.

GOT TO MOVE
(Homesick James Williamson)

FADED UP in the middle of a sequence, this is a mid-tempo blues with some acoustic and distorted slide and another tedious vocal by Spencer. The arrangement has a few stops-and-starts for dynamic variation. It's a pity Green didn't take a lead solo on this. Another track that thankfully rides off into the sunset before too long.

Mr Wonderful

UK Blue Horizon 7-63205 August 1968; not released in US;
reissued UK Castle Communications ESSLP 010 (1989);
UK CD Castle Communications ESSCD 010 (1989)

ON THEIR SECOND ALBUM, FLEETWOOD MAC CONTINUED TO EXPLORE THEIR own fairly authentic take on the blues, but with greater strength than they had mustered on their début. *Mr Wonderful* was recorded in four days with no rehearsals. However, some of the problems which were noticeable on the first LP crop up again.

Jeremy Spencer's Elmore James impersonation soon becomes irksome and compromises the quality of the songs. By contrast, Green sounds confident and plays in a more extroverted manner than before. The band's sound is quietly enhanced by piano parts supplied by Christine Perfect who married John McVie in August 1968. She would be crucial to the vast success of the band's remodelled mid-Seventies line-up. There is also a horn section consisting of Johnnie Almond, Steve Gregory, Dave Howard and Rolan Vaughan, with Tony 'Duster' Bennett on harmonica. Apparently, as with the first album, Spencer does not play on any of the Green tracks. By this time the Mac had cut 'Black Magic Woman' but this was only available as a single.

STOP MESSIN' ROUND
(Green/Adams)

THE ALBUM starts with a more sophisticated sound in which Green's lead has the support of piano and a horn section. Green sounds ebullient and more confident on this track, switching tone on his guitar for the second break. The third verse comes with 4 bars of stops before the rhythm picks up again. Although there is piano on the track, it is mixed quite a way down and is thus tricky to hear. Green's lead guitar plays predominantly on the major pentatonic scale and ends with a strongly hit chord for a dramatic finish. This was on the band's *Greatest Hits*.

I'VE LOST MY BABY
(J. Spencer)

FOR THIS track the drums are mixed back, the piano sounds like it's across the road, and the bass is much further up front. There are horns here too but you can hardly hear them. This is a medium slow tempo E blues with the vocal and slide phrases by Spencer. If all blues were like this, it would be little wonder that their women were leaving the poor bluesmen. There are some intonation problems as well as the strange mix. There are no dynamic changes to help either, it just trundles along at the same level all the way. 'I've lost my baby'... well, try another riff, man.

ROLLIN' MAN
(Green/Adams)

THIS IS much better, with Green trading licks with the horn section and stopping suddenly at the end of the first 12 bars. 'Rollin' Man' has a pleasing swing to it and is quite a faithful recreation of an American blues. It doesn't have the fire and arrogance of Clapton, but there's a pleasing poetry and joy to Green's playing here. He sounds as exuberant as on 'Stop Messin' Round'. Towards the end they go into 12/8 and a quicker tempo, and turn up the heat, as Green plays away in true Bluesbreakers style. There's one piercing high note just at the fade which is a delight.

DUST MY BROOM
(James/Josea)

FINALLY, after re-writing Elmore James, Spencer gets down to doing a cover of the Real Thing. He certainly knows how to play that riff, and at least here it doesn't sound as sludgy as on his own tracks. The performance is supported by piano and spare horns and keeps up the tempo and upbeat feel established by the earlier tracks.

LOVE THAT BURNS
(Green/Adams)

THIS IS a slow A minor 12-bar in 12/8 with a mournful horn part, and is mostly carried by the piano and horns and the rhythm section. Green keeps his guitar playing very sparse, often going many bars before interjecting a phrase or two and often tailing away with a flurry of very quiet notes. This type of blues acted as the inspiration for Led Zeppelin's 'Tea For One'. It would be nice to have heard a bit more of the tumbling piano phrases that occur every now and again. This is very much a lachrymose slow-burner. There's a palpable sense of relief when Green finally takes a solo, although he never lets rip, thus maintaining the tension – one of his strongest characteristics as a guitar player. It ends with a slow fade and a piano break. This was included on the 1971 *Greatest Hits*.

DOCTOR BROWN
(Brown)

Or 'DUST My Broom (Slight Return)'. In which Spencer has another opportunity to play that riff and employ those irritating vocal mannerisms while the band clump their way around another 12-bar. Listen out for the saxes in the background – the stars of a not very good show.

NEED YOUR LOVE TONIGHT
(J. Spencer)

Or 'WOKE Up This Morning Playing The Same Song'. By some unaccountable dereliction of group responsibility, the Mac allowed this track to come straight after the previous, another 'Dust My Broom'-pastiche by Spencer in the same key, at the same tempo, and with the same riff!

Spencer links every lyric cliché in the book. You may think your hi-fi is on 'repeat' mode. Or you may find yourself praying for the Children of God to come a little sooner...

IF YOU BE MY BABY
(Green/Adams)

A MEDIUM-slow D major 12/8 blues in which Green once more trades licks with the horn section with that distinctive 'nasal' tone from his Les Paul. The guitar work lifts it above the average (Green has several breaks before the fade) but the track as a whole comes across as merely average.

EVENIN' BOOGIE
(J. Spencer)

A FAST 12/8 blues in which Spencer attempts to trade slide chords with the brass section. The effect is a little messy. There's a sax break at one point. Taking an extended solo somewhat exposes the limitations of Spencer's slide technique. Slide guitar is a style of playing easy to make a great sound on for about 50 seconds. After that, it sorts out them that really know from the bluffers. Here pretty soon the ideas run out. But at least he doesn't sing.

LAZY POKER BLUES
(Green/Adams)

ANOTHER uptempo jump blues in 12/8 with Green lyrically exploring a ribald metaphor involving the phallic connotations of pokers and fires (ain't nuthin to do with cards, y'all). One of Green's most ebullient performances on the album with regard to the lead work.

COMING HOME
(Elmore James)

OR ELMORE James recycling himself as recycled by Spencer. It's that riff again, and guess what? She Dun 'im Wrong. Mid-tempo, same key, same fret – you get the picture. It's only the fourth or fifth time on this platter. But it is short. It is a little known fact that the first draft of Reverend Martin Luther King's speech "I have a dream" actually continued "that that son of a gun will find another riff!!!"

TRYING SO HARD TO FORGET
(Green/Adams)

THE ALBUM closes with this slow, gentle, introverted blues in E with guitar and harmonica, the latter played by Tony 'Duster' Bennett, a friend of Green. You'll have to turn the volume up on this one because it's all recorded quite quietly. It brings the album to a subdued close. The lyrics refer to Green's early life growing up in Whitechapel in the East End of London.

The Pious Bird Of Good Omen

US Not released; UK Blue Horizon 7-63215, released August 1969; reissued UK CBS 32050 (1981) with different sleeve

AFTER THE RELEASE OF *MR WONDERFUL*, THE BAND RECRUITED A THIRD guitarist, Danny Kirwan. Green was apparently uncomfortable with so much limelight and wanted someone with whom to share it. The move may also have indicated that the chemistry between Spencer and Green wasn't quite right. Green saw Kirwan playing in London with a band called Boilerhouse. He looked good and played nervy lead guitar. With three guitarists, Fleetwood Mac now had a new range of musical possibilities. The question was, would they do anything with them?

At the end of 1968, 'Albatross' became a huge hit, increasing the band's fame. Their contract with Blue Horizon came to an end and they signed a one-off deal with ex-Rolling Stones manager Andrew Loog Oldham's Immediate records. This led to the single 'Man Of The World', the flip side of which had 'Someone's Gonna Get Their Head Kicked In Tonight' credited to Earl Vince and The Valiants, the pseudonym coined by Jeremy Spencer for his Fifties rock'n'roll pastiches. This must make the 'Man Of The World' single one of the most schizophrenic in the history of rock.

The band had evolved an extraordinary live act, full of innuendo, with the result that they were getting banned from gigs. Condoms full of milk were hung off guitars or thrown at the audience. Fleetwood describes them as "a funny, vulgar, vaudeville blues band at that time, playing music as much to amuse ourselves as please an audience and make money". Crucial to all the larking about was Spencer, who invested in a gold lamé suit in order to imitate Elvis. According to Fleetwood, Spencer was "a compulsive parodist, a gifted mimic, a kind of ultimate imitator... eventually our stage show would divide into half blues jams and half Jeremy's Fifties pop parodies".

The Pious Bird Of Good Omen was really a compilation of Mac recordings, rather than a proper new studio album. It lifted songs from the first two albums and included with them the two hit singles 'Albatross' and 'Black Magic Woman'. Those tracks made it plain that the musical tensions in the band might prove too much to reconcile. Fleetwood Mac obviously had it in them to be so much more than a blues band. Spencer's songs in particular simply wilt before the brilliance of the two Green singles, which could now be played live thanks to the recruiting of third guitarist Danny Kirwan. The identity was beginning to fracture.

In the US this album was anticipated by one called 'English Rose', released in January 1969 (Epic BN 26446). Track-listing was: Stop Messin' Round', 'Jigsaw Puzzle Blues', 'Doctor Brown', 'Something Inside Of Me', 'Evenin' Boogie', 'Love That Burns', 'Black Magic Woman', 'I've Lost My Baby', 'One Sunny Day', 'Without You', 'Coming Home', 'Albatross. It was re-issued in the US (as Columbia CSP P11651) in 1973.

NEED YOUR LOVE SO BAD
(Little Willie John)

GREEN WAS inspired to put strings on this after hearing B.B.King's version. This is a slow 8-bar blues whose chord sequence gave Green plenty of opportunity to play some expressive guitar, though to his credit he resists the temptation to overplay. The arrangement is delicate, the strings sweet on the ear, and the McVie,' Fleetwood rhythm section steady throughout. Green turns in a fine vocal performance on this, one of Mac's best blues covers. Listen for the reverb on the guitar on the opposite side of the mix towards the end of the song. This was re-released as a single in 1969 and included on the *Greatest Hits*.

RAMBLING PONY
(P.A. Green)

THIS IS the closest Green ever got to Hendrix, recalling in particular the Cherokee beat of Hendrix's 'Izabella' and 'Love Or Confusion'. A bass drum keeps a North American Indian beat going, supported by harmonica, while the guitar plays the melody and a minor pentatonic riff between the vocals. A chorus of distant male voices supports Green's in a kind of tribal harmony.

THE BIG BOAT
(E. Boyd)

THE LEAD vocal is taken by Eddie Boyd, while in the back of this short, authentically smokey Chicago mix are the rhythm section, a boogie piano (played by Boyd), and Green's guitar fills. Green's solo on this, while not as fierce as Hendrix, certainly recalls the solo on 'Red House', presumably drawing on the same source of Buddy Guy *et al*.

I BELIEVE MY TIME AIN'T LONG
(J. Spencer)

THIS IS the latest in Spencer's takes on Elmore James and 'Dust My Broom', commencing with a verse that lyrically borrows from that song. The remainder of the track is just like any other Jeremy Spencer track you may have heard.

THE SUN IS SHINING
(J. Spencer)

ANOTHER ghastly overwrought Spencer song, this time in slow 12/8, complete with piano glissandos, slide fills (but not 'Dust My Broom', phew!) and a highly mannered vocal which occasionally goes off-piste from the ski-slopes of even blue-note singing. Somewhere there is a blues band playing in a club or pub very near you who sound just like this...

ALBATROSS
(P.A. Green)

SIDE TWO of the LP kicks off with one of the most famous rock instrumentals ever and a slice of pure genius. 'Albatross' was allegedly inspired by a Fifties record by Santo and Johnny called 'Sleepwalk'. The story goes that Green was flying from New York to London and the main tune kept going through his mind as he looked out of the window. He was also thinking about Samuel Taylor Coleridge's haunted poem *The Rhyme of the Ancient Mariner* in which an albatross killed by the sailors brings down on them a terrible curse. 'Albatross' is one of those tracks that you think you know and of which you have a just estimate, until you listen to it again and find how unnervingly good it is.

The New Bond Street studios offered a cavernous recording area whose ambient sound was vital to the feel of the track. Green described the number as "like a whole lifetime in three minutes, flying out and away". Producer Mike Vernon has given eloquent praise to Green's guitar-playing on this: "Peter was one of those rare musicians who play only what is necessary and no more. Listening to 'Albatross' now, you know that the feel of the man was absolutely incredible, unrivalled... but you also know that he only played what was needed."

Green's guitar plays the main tune, soaked in reverb and increasingly counterpointed by harmonised slide guitar parts on either side of the stereo mix. Kirwan played the second slide part on his Telecaster. In turn they are answered by a distant high slide part. At one point that very high slide has two phrases to itself. Mick Fleetwood keeps the tune mesmerising with gently struck toms and splashes of cymbals like flashes of sun off the sea, while McVie just adds the requisite root notes. Rarely

has a rock band been so on top of its arrangement and managed to rein back its collective ego to let the music breathe. You have to go forward to some of The Police's *Synchronicity* material to find such careful playing. Green carries the main tune with consummate taste, so much so that the track leaves the arena of what we think of as 'rock' music to attain heights that are quite something else. From here on Green's musical vision was clearly going to lead the band away from 12-bar blues. After writing it, Green said he knew it would be a hit, and it was, topping the charts. The Beatles paid it the ultimate homage by trying to emulate its sunny feel on 'Sun King' from *Abbey Road*.

'Albatross' was re-released as a single in May 1973 on CBS, and was a massive hit again. It came out in February 1989 on a 12" or CD, with 'Man Of The World' and 'Black Magic Woman'. In 1990 it appeared in the Old Gold series with 'Need Your Love So Bad' on the flip.

BLACK MAGIC WOMAN
(P.A. Green)

THE DOUBLE-punch. With a high shimmering minor 7, Green produces a D minor 12-bar variant and gets another hit. This was made famous in the US by Santana, who exploited the slinky, sexy potential of the song. Green turns in one of his most melodic solos, climbing up and down the minor chords, tumbling over and over in the reverb like a soul falling into the pit. Yet again the rhythm section came up trumps – Fleetwood with an eccentric rhythm and McVie with his wandering bass lines. The coda doubles the tempo and swings to the finish. This was inspired partly by Green's girlfriend of the time, Sandra Elsdon, and Otis Rush's 'All Your Loving'.

JUST THE BLUES
(E. Boyd)

THE SECOND of two tracks cut with Boyd on vocals and piano. This is a slow restrained blues performance, despite the initial flourish of piano. The arrangement is sparse, and Green looks for the gaps on the left side of the mix, playing some subdued phrases in a supporting role to Boyd's vocal. There are some great bends by Green, complementing the held-in sensuality of the lyric. When the solo comes, Green elects to commence with some

major phrases and tends to keep it that way, while Boyd turns in some jazzy piano. The net result is a relatively sophisticated performance that refuses to be hurried or bounced into any theatrics.

JIGSAW PUZZLE BLUES
(D. Kirwan)

THE MAC'S new recruit gets one of his songs recorded. It starts with a heavy accented four-to-the-bar beat before launching into a major key 12-bar with a few key tricks and time shifts and a section in a minor key. It's an instrumental track, on which Kirwan's lead guitar has a heavier, wiry vibrato and a thinner tone than Green's.

The Pious Bird Of Good Omen also includes 'Looking For Somebody' from *Peter Green's Fleetwood Mac*, and 'Coming Home' and 'Stop Messin' Round' from *Mr Wonderful*.

Then Play On

US Reprise RS 6368 (October 1969); UK Reprise RSLP 9000 (September 1969); Reissued UK reprise K 44103 (1971); US CD Reprise 6368 2 (1988); UK CD WEA 927448 2 (1988)

GREEN WAS BECOMING INCREASINGLY FRUSTRATED WITH THE BAND PLAYING blues and Fifties parodies, and wanted to play more improvised music. The presence of Danny Kirwan at gigs helped this to some degree, and he was told he could have half the songs on the next record. Fleetwood remembers: "We didn't want to release any more records with Jeremy singing Elmore James, so Jeremy didn't even play on it."

Released only a short while after *The Pious Bird of Good Omen*, this was to be Peter Green's last album with Fleetwood Mac. It shows a clear evolution from their earlier repertoire: here is a band finding its musical identity, and developing innovative instrumental approaches and textures. With new producer Martin Birch, the band used more overdubbing than on the earlier albums. Christine Perfect was also involved in the sessions.

The stand-out track is the epic 'Oh Well', with 'Before The Beginning' coming a short way behind.

This was a top five album in the UK and a commercial success in the US, where it became the first of the band's records to sell more than 100,000 copies. *Then Play On* is the best studio album that Fleetwood Mac made in their first incarnation, and deserves to be included in any list of the best albums of 1969.

The first US issue omitted 'One Sunny Day' and 'Without You', and on the second US release 'One Sunny Day', 'Without You', 'When You Say' and 'My Dream' were omitted, with 'Oh Well Parts 1 & 2' added.

COMING YOUR WAY
(D. Kirwan)

THIS TRACK opens in an exotic vein, with the band following the style set by their earlier instrumentals, and twin guitars playing in B minor on either side. After a vocal overshadowed by guitars, the opening theme is reiterated. A bass playing straight eights, and the fast conga playing throughout, create a throbbing rhythm reminiscent of Santana. When the distorted guitar plays a short break after the first verse, the comparison seems even more apposite. Toward the end there's another guitar solo over a slower tempo, supported by several guitar parts. This sounds like the starting point for Wishbone Ash.

A good example of the Mac doing something fresh with the 12-bar heritage.

CLOSING MY EYES
(P.A. Green)

SOME interesting guitar and bass arrangements feature in the quiet, reflective opening to 'Closing My Eyes', a song in which the vocal is a tale of love and loneliness sung by Green.

There are no drums on the track except some tom-tom fills. The arrangement is delicate, with harmonised descending guitars and a nylon classical lead line at various points. This is a song in the mould of 'Man Of The World', though without that track's dynamic pick-up in the middle. Excellent use is made of reverb to give a dark depth to the guitar parts. Toward the end the drums pound away for a few bars and create a feel which briefly suggests Sixties West Coast band Love.

SHOW-BIZ BLUES
(P.A. Green)

THIS STARTS with solo slide guitar before turning into a fast tempo 12-bar in what sounds like an open tuning (probably open E). Hand-claps and tambourine provide the rhythm. The track is a throwback to the band's blues origins. There's a nice unpredictability to the changes during this 12-bar derivation. The lyrics reflect Green's disillusionment with his stardom and refer to life on the road and, in the ironic last verse, feature a pun on his name: "You're sitting there so green, but man, I'm the same as you". It fades away on a single slide note.

MY DREAM
(D. Kirwan)

THIS IS A mid-tempo instrumental with a pleasing descending chord progression and some unusual chord shifts with guitar parts spread about the stereo image. The tune owes something to Hank Marvin's 'Playing With The Shadows' in the way in which it moves around those chords. The drums are perhaps a little far back in the mix, but it's a pleasant number.

UNDERWAY
(P.A. Green)

'UNDERWAY' was one of several tracks that evolved from long jam sessions. This begins tentatively with a dreamy major sixth chord layered over by guitar fills, a sound which creates a languid mood which is never really undermined by the continuous drum fills and slashing distorted chords in its centre. Green initially picks out his melody on the right. Echo is added just before the fade on parts of the guitar line.

This track is from the 'Albatross' songbook, and is good but not essential.

OH WELL
(P.A. Green)

THIS WAS the band's most ambitious recording, though it has been called a Peter Green solo track in all but name. Part 1 became a hit single.

A bluesy acoustic riff played by Green on a Michigan dobro-style resonator guitar is quickly picked up by massed electrics, which then move into a standard hard rock riff in E, at different octaves. Guitars climb up the scale before a cowbell is left alone to accompany the disillusioned lyric of the verse. After the riff, the band launch into a full-on triple guitar assault, the lead lines battling to be heard until the sudden stop. The drums then thump through the riff section once more.

Before long, the noise has subsided into the much longer Part 2 which is led by a Ramirez Spanish guitar playing chords, and an electric guitar playing low down melodies reminiscent of Duane Eddy. There is also a recorder part to add to the atmosphere. Anger has subsided into bleak withdrawal. The sadness in Green's music is present again, and makes Part 1 seem a long time ago.

Being utterly uncompromising in his presentation, Green insisted on buying himself a Cello and teaching himself how to play it in order to get exactly the cello sound which he wanted on this track. The flute was played by his girlfriend Sandra Elsdon.

There's a piano toward the end before the resolution on to a major chord, which fades away to leave the Spanish guitar and cello. Many guitarists would have been tempted to solo over this section, but Green is again reticent and leaves the melody to speak for itself. The final section is dramatically turned by the drums into a sort of funereal march.

Part 1 of the track has a memorable tune, and consequently worked well live. To Green's frustration, Part 2, which he considered superior, did not. By now Green's musical vision was undermining his ability to communicate with his fellow band members, and there were battles within Fleetwood Mac over how this track should be recorded.

The rhythm section bet Green £5 that Part 1 wouldn't be a hit. It was.

ALTHOUGH THE SUN IS SHINING
(D. Kirwan)

THE ACOUSTIC guitars of this short, lovelorn ballad come in effectively after the previous track. There are some unusual guitar fills here, some odd vocal harmonies from Kirwan, and a cheery chorus which sounds like The Small Faces slowed down and gone mainstream.

RATTLESNAKE SHAKE
(P.A. Green)

A SLOW heavy blues whose lyrics concern self-instigated sexual pleasures. Green's guitar is much more strident here, possibly as a result of the example set by heavier bands, notably Led Zeppelin who were making considerable waves throughout 1969.

It's a slow burner of a track with layered guitars and a restrained lead from Green. This was selected for the *Greatest Hits*. It would've been interesting to hear what Hendrix could've made of it.

SEARCHING FOR MADGE
(J.G. McVie)

THIS IS AN instrumental written by bass player John McVie, the ideas for which came from jamming. It begins with some pile-driving playing by the rhythm section on one chord.

There's a sudden break and fading away after a minute or so, then the track comes back. Listening on headphones reveals intriguing bits of studio trickery, such as guitars panned from one side to the other, and the addition of reverb at various points. The momentum never really lets up – the track is reminiscent of Santana at their most driving. Towards the end there's an extraordinary piece of string music, after some solo guitar stabs and studio laughter, which could easily be U2 on their *Passengers* project. Then the driving blues comes back for the third time. It's an enjoyable journey – you never know what's next. The Madge of this and the following track was a fan from Darlington who followed the band all over the country.

It is ironic that, having written the track, McVie ends up playing on a single note for most of it.

FIGHTING FOR MADGE
(M.J.K Fleetwood)

MORE JAMMING salvaged by the noble art of tape-splicing. The tempo is that of a medium one-chord blues, before the band accelerate and get into a driving groove reminiscent of the previous track. Kirwan and Green begin by trading phrases, before Green takes the main part of the soloing. Kirwan later takes over with a vibrato laden solo, which wanders around the stereo mix. This is a shorter piece, which fades to laughter at the end.

WHEN YOU SAY
(D. Kirwan)

ANOTHER slow acoustic ballad with Kirwan's voice double-tracked and ghosted by various guitar lines. There are no drums on this, but McVie offers a simple bass line to support the chords. It's a love-song with a few interesting twists in the sequence. The la-la section drags a bit and seems rather po-faced. It's not one of the album's stronger tracks, but is preferable (just) to 'Dust My Broom' take 3,000 – despite the plodding rhythm which drags after a while. It's too long at 4:22 and would have been better cut back. This would only have really worked if sung in a thoroughly camp way by Freddie Mercury of Queen. It was also recorded by Christine Perfect on her 1970 solo album.

LIKE CRYING
(D. Kirwan)

AN OPEN tuning excursion with harmonised voices through a 12-bar derivative. Again, quite an anticipation of Wishbone Ash. No drums or bass on this brief drifting excursion, just two guitars, one open-tuned rhythm, the other playing lead phrases. The message is that the woman has got the blues!

BEFORE THE BEGINNING
(P.A Green)

A LOVELY jaw-dropping intro ushers in another slow Green blues in B flat minor, an unusual key for guitar music. Some beautiful tumbling double-stops give way to a verse supported by an excellent bass line and subtle kettle-drum playing by Fleetwood. The track is made all the better by the strongly accented parts where the chords are hit in straight eights. Along the way there's loads of fine guitar work, and trademark touches of echo. The intro guitar phrase gets reprised just before the fade, which really comes too early. You can't help wishing that Green had taken an opportunity to solo here. The tune started in B flat minor but by a stroke of creative genius, Green reprises it in G minor, a tone and a half lower, giving the coda an odd sense of dislocation. Green told me in 1997 that this track was one of his favourites, and that the lyrics were concerned with the Buddhist idea of reincarnation. It is nothing short of a minor masterpiece.

You must have *Then Play On* if only for this track!

Blues Jam In Chicago

US Blue Horizon (Vol.1 Bh 4803. Vol.2 Bh 4805) December 1969; UK Blue Horizon 7-66227 December 1969.
US release was as two separate albums

THIS DOUBLE ALBUM CAME AS A RESULT OF RECORDING SESSIONS AT THE Chess Ter-Mar Studios, Chicago, in January 1969. Late in 1968, producer Mike Vernon had been considering getting the band to record with some of the giants of US blues in the city that had spawned so much quintessential blues. The Mac were booked for a short US tour over the end of 1968 and the start of 1969. They played a gig at the Regal Theater in Chicago opening for Muddy Waters. Willie Dixon drew up a short-list of black musicians willing and able to play with the band. They included Otis Spann, Walter 'Shakey' Horton, S.P. Leary, J.T Brown, Buddy Guy (under the alias of 'Guitar Buddy'), and David "Honeyboy" Edwards. Otis Spann was the half brother of Muddy Waters and someone that Green admired, and Spencer was delighted at the presence of J.T Brown, tenor player for Elmore James.

The atmosphere was a little tense at first, but Fleetwood recalls, "As soon as Peter's respect for their music became apparent, they stopped treating us like tourists." The recording was done over a two-day period with freezing weather outside. Studio chat, the buzz of the amps and engineer's comments add to the live-in-the-studio atmosphere. You get false intros and after-take comments. The title *Blues Jam* is certainly apposite for what is going on, and as long as your expectations aren't too high and you like the blues you'll like this – all 100 minutes of it. Since this was released after *Then Play On* it may have made some people wonder where the band was going. Fleetwood Mac had left Blue Horizon by this time, but couldn't prevent the release, which Green was unhappy about.

VOLUME 1

WATCH OUT
(P.A. Green)

THE ALBUM starts with a medium-paced instrumental during which Green gradually shifts into a fiercer tone from the guitar supported by the rhythm section. With a rhythm guitar sliding round dominant ninth chords, Green warns his woman to watch out for him. After the last verse Green makes a temporary shift up to the high notes before snapping out a last run and, ending unexpectedly.

OOH BABY
(Chester Burnett)

STUDIO talk enhances the atmosphere, with Mick Fleetwood doing a brief Motown bass drum improvisation. This is another medium-paced blues based on an ascending riff with the occasional fill on guitar. Green solos using the sliding sixths figures which feature most famously on 'Killing Floor' and would turn up at increased velocity on Led Zeppelin's 'Lemon Song'.

SOUTH INDIANA TAKE 1
(W. Horton)

ANOTHER 12-bar in E, this time with Walter 'Shakey' Horton on harmonica and guitars taking the lead breaks.

SOUTH INDIANA TAKE 2
(W. Horton)

THEY DECIDED to have another go at this. The intro has the band working out how they're going to start it. Take 2 features a heavier guitar sound than its predecessor.

LAST NIGHT
(W. Jacobs)

THIS IS A slow blues with harmonica flourishes and a spidery single note riff played in unison by the guitar and bass. Green takes the vocal, telling the story of how he lost the best friend he ever had. One of the better tracks, with the virtue of restraint.

RED HOT JAM
(P.A. Green)

THE ENGINEER announces a Green instrumental, complemented by Horton's harmonica, and no less than three guitarists – Green, Buddy Guy and Honey Boy Edwards – and blues legend Willie Dixon on upright bass. It's a sprightly track if a little messy in the arrangement, and the tuning problems are sometimes apparent. Dixon can be heard talking at the end.

I'M WORRIED
(E. James)

THE FIRST of four consecutive tracks with Jeremy Spencer at the helm, leading off with three Elmore James covers. On performances Spencer is supported by J.T. Brown on sax, Kirwan, Dixon and Fleetwood. It must have been a nervous moment, playing the blues in this kind of company in Chess studios, but to give him credit, Spencer rises to the occasion with a spirited, nervy performance.

I HELD MY BABY LAST NIGHT
(E. James)

WITH HARDLY a pause Spencer takes them into this slower track. You can hear from the opening bars that everyone's not entirely sure what they're doing, but after a while it settles down. Spencer's reverb-laden Gibson semi-acoustic is here played with subdued feeling, he takes care not to fire all his shots too early – which is pretty essential in a slow blues like this. A blues about a breakdown in communication between lovers.

MADISON BLUES
(E. James)

LATER TO be the title of a live Fleetwood Mac album, 'Madison Blues' commences with the engineer asking for the tuning to be corrected. With little more than a sudden 12th fret blast, this uptempo blues gets underway. The guitar and sax work well together on this. Spencer loosens up a little and vocally introduces some of the mannerisms that make his studio recordings so irritating on the early Fleetwood albums.

I CAN'T HOLD OUT
(E. James)

A MEDIUM-paced blues with a tricky timed intro, and stop chords through the first four-bars. Spencer punctuates the song with 12-fret 'Dust My Broom' riffs. This is the chunkiest of the cuts.

I NEED YOUR LOVE
(Rogers)

FOR THIS uptempo blues, Horton takes the vocal and supplies the harmonica, while Otis Spann plays piano in sprightly fashion, with a variety of 16ths and glissandos, and trading licks with the harmonica. Green and Kirwan supply the rhythm guitars, and S.P.Leary gives Mick Fleetwood a break from the drums. One of the better tracks with a fine dynamic ending.

I GOT THE BLUES
(W. Horton)

PLAYED BY the same line-up as the previous track. Harmonica and piano lead the abrupt intro to this slower 12-bar variant with unpredictable timing on the chord changing through the first verse. Horton's vocal gives 'I Got The Blues' a moody but warm feeling.

VOLUME 2

WORLD'S IN A TANGLE
(J. Lane)

THIS MEDIUM-paced blues leaves Danny Kirwan to solo and sing lead, taking over from 'Shakey' Horton at the mike. There's a momentary hiatus where the drums stop for a few bars at the start. Otis Spann's piano tends to outshine everything else. The lyric stands out because Kirwan talks about going into the army and wiping out the 'Reds'. You may take it as satirical...or you may not.

Kirwan's vocal is shown up as lacking the quality of the other vocals on the sessions, and his lead work certainly doesn't have the depth of Green's.

TALK WITH YOU
(D. Kirwan)

MICK FLEETWOOD gets back on the drum stool for this, Kirwan's second vocal on his own composition, which deals with man/woman issues, let us say, especially in the matter of shared finances. After two verses there's a pleasing instrumental break with some unison playing between the instruments which makes some of the melodic lines jump out.

LIKE IT THIS WAY
(D. Kirwan)

THIS HAS a false start which breaks down, probably because one of the guitarists decides to change his tone. Green and Kirwan echo each other's phrases in an effective call-and-answer routine, while Otis Spann supplies some rollicking piano. There are three verses before Kirwan opens the vocal, with the guitars supplying fills in between the lines of lyric. It sounds occasionally messy, and sometimes it seems like the piano isn't keeping up with the changing chords. However, as a whole it has plenty of energy.

SOMEDAY SOON BABY
(O. Spann)

OTIS SPANN takes the mike to sing his own song. It starts with a guitar solo passage which Green almost stops, but Spann tells him to keep playing and after 12 bars the rest of the band come in. Spann leads proceedings from the piano with a forceful vocal with plenty of authority. Green continues playing sparse fills while Kirwan plays quiet chords in the background. This is a long, slow, subdued blues. With a "well, all right!" Spann invites Green to take a solo in the middle, whilst adding a few phrases on the piano, after which Spann invites 'Lucia' (the lady in question) to come home to him. At seven minutes it is, perhaps, a little long, but the last verse has an effective change of dynamics, using the stop-chord tactic before a rousing ending.

HUNGRY COUNTRY GIRL
(O. Spann)

ONE OF THE more eccentric items on offer, this features a creeping stop-note riff over which Spann talks his way through the first verse, explaining about the relationship between women who can't help themselves and the necessity of feeding farm animals. From there on he hollers his way through the song, while the band carry on with the riff. Spann occasionally sounds like he's practising for the annual singers' Bust-A-Mike contest. The solo here is taken by Spann on the piano.

BLACK JACK BLUES
(J.T. Brown)

THERE'S another change of line-up. J.T. Brown sings a song about losing all his money in a card game, while Dixon plays seriously out-of-tune upright bass, Spencer supplies slide guitar and Honey Boy Edwards adds guitar. The track provides a different colour from anything that's gone before. The lyric is much more a story than some of the others and holds the song together. The solo is taken by Brown on sax with a few phrases from Spencer thrown in. The song has a happy ending with Brown winning $500. At the end Brown complains that the key was too low – whether for his voice or sax isn't clear.

EVERY DAY I HAVE THE BLUES
(P. Chaiman)

SPENCER returns to the mike to sing this number and play slide, with Brown blowing sax, Green supporting on rhythm guitar, and Honey Boy Edwards somewhere in the back of the mix. Spencer manages not to over-play his Elmore James riff and turns in a reasonable vocal. Toward the end of the song his slide playing introduces some interestingly unconventional notes which stand out among the straight blues harmony.

ROCKIN' BOOGIE
(J. Spencer)

THIS IS AN instrumental taken at a frenetic pace, one of the fastest tracks on the whole session. Spencer takes two 12-bars to solo and then lets Brown play a solo on sax which is aptly described by the title. Mick Fleetwood gets into another splendidly locomotive groove to drive the whole thing along and Dixon adds some strange percussion sounds from the upright bass before the whole thing comes to an unrehearsed sudden ending.

SUGAR MAMA
(Williamson)

THIS MUSCULAR blues starts with Green tugging the leg of producer Mike Vernon and then with take three launching explosively into its great intro. This take flounders, as does another after only a few seconds, before they finally settle into it. Green takes the vocal and plays some mean guitar, with Spencer sitting this one out. Green uses a much heavier, aggressive vibrato on the guitar, approximating more to a Buddy Guy style of playing. The vocal is good, and, overall, this is one of the best tracks on the session.

HOMEWORK
(Clark, Perkins)

THE FINAL track is an uptempo minor blues, a nod back to Fifties rock'n'roll and not a 12-bar at all. The switch of form is striking after so much 12-bar and makes the song sound positively Byzantine in complexity. Both vocally and in the guitar tone, Green sounds quite a lot like Clapton here, and it's not difficult to imagine Cream covering this track.

Kiln House

US Reprise RS 6408 September 1970; UK Reprise RSLP 9004
September 1970; reissued UK Reprise K 5400 1 (1971);
US CD reprise 6408 2; UK CD WEA 927453 2

FLEETWOOD HAD LONG BEEN AWARE THAT PETER GREEN WAS NOT A HAPPY MAN. Looking back on the 'Man Of The World' single, he said: "In retrospect we should have seen it as a warning of what was coming." At one point, Green said to his drummer: "Mick, I wasn't cut out for success. I can take this business or leave it." He was tired of playing the same songs and was feeling guilty about the band's money, often trying to talk the band into giving most of their income to charity. The final crisis came during a European tour in 1970. He had taken a number of LSD trips in 1969 and was becoming more religious in outlook – a change expressed in the clothes he was wearing on stage. In Munich he spent several days with some German hippies who were into acid and counter-culture ways of looking at things. They even followed him back to London. That was the straw that broke the camel's back.

On 11 April 1970, Peter Green announced that he was quitting the band, though contracts obliged him to complete a number of dates. In May the single 'Green Manalishi' was released and made the UK Top 10. In many respects this was a classic note on which to bow out, the turbulence of the track perfectly mirroring the inner conflict which caused him to quit. Green played his last gig as a member of Fleetwood Mac on 25 May at the Lyceum in London. He went on to record a solo album of impromptu sessions called *The End Of The Game* and two singles 'Heavy Heart' and 'Beast of Burden'.

Deprived of the band's musical leader, Fleetwood Mac made the decision to carry on. In reality, the triple guitar Fleetwood Mac was now in slow burn-up re-entry mode. As they burned out, they managed a couple more albums. *Kiln House*, with artwork by Christine McVie, was largely a Spencer/Kirwan project. It was named after the country house in Hampshire where the band reconvened to live and continue working in best late Sixties Let's-Get-It-Together-In-The-Country mode. Mick Fleetwood believes it stopped the band disintegrating altogether, though at times they did come perilously close to giving up. Fleetwood remembers one night where everyone announced they were quitting and he talked them back in, one by one. The work pace was leisurely and *Kiln House* is a bit like a rudderless ship. Spencer offered some Fifties rock'n'roll mixed with some more experimental features but the band were struggling to find a voice of their own. Christine McVie was not credited on the original sleeve, nor for her drawing of it. It was not a commercial success.

THIS IS THE ROCK
(Spencer)

THIS IS A mid-tempo slice of country rock in a slight Elvis mode, with Spencer copying The Jordanaires, and with just the right Fifties reverb on his voice. There are acoustic guitars, light electrics and light drumming. Spencer and Kirwan are certainly no match for Scotty Moore and, like so many imitations of Fifties rock, this comes over as watered-down, too studied and self-conscious. Preferable to Shakin' Stevens, I'll grant you, but not by much.

STATION MAN
(Kirwan/Spencer/J.McVie)

THIS FADES in, with block vocals taking the verse, and slide phrases in between. There's a muffled heavy guitar riff that recalls the figure at the end of the verses in 'Oh Well'. Christine McVie's voice is evident in the block harmony. Reminiscent in parts of Neil Young, it tends to lack attack, although the more it goes on, the more distorted the guitars start to get, especially so on the second guitar solo (which sounds like Paul Kossoff of Free). The lyrics don't do much more than play around with some standard blues images about trains of love and being a station man and waiting. The track is too long at 5:49. On the fade-out there's some nice lead, possibly from Kirwan.

BLOOD ON THE FLOOR
(Spencer)

THIS IS A maudlin tongue-in-cheek country and western song of a man about to be executed, sung by Spencer in a lugubrious fake-southern US accent. It is supported by the appropriate backing vocals and has the appropriate brief key-change at the end of the bridge. Clearly satirical, it's for country stations and insomniacs only.

HI HO SILVER
(Fats Waller)

THIS IS better, a 12-bar with a driving drum-beat, inane lyrics and distorted guitars and harmonica. Spencer has voices going 'bop-bop' in the background and occasionally tries to put shades of Little Richard and Buddy Holly into the vocal. In the middle he takes a slide solo and there are piano glissandos as you would expect. Nothing to do with Jeff Beck's 'Hi Ho Silver Lining'.

JEWEL EYED JUDY
(Kirwan)

GUITAR arpeggios, low electric piano and a three-chord change give this a slight feel of late Beatles/Badfinger. Kirwan takes the lead vocal, double-tracked. The chorus is more forceful with an extra buzzy rhythm guitar coming in, and you could imagine McCartney belting its lyric. It then slips back into the languid groove of the verse. It certainly has dynamic shifts from verse into the chorus, and, as a result, is one of the stronger tracks. The track is named after band friend Judy Wong, one of the 'faces' of the flower-power era in London.

BUDDY'S SONG
(Spencer)

SPENCER allegedly donated the royalties on this to Buddy Holly's mother. It's another exercise in pastiche with the band conjuring up the thumping drums of Holly & The Crickets, complete with the basic fast strumming of three chords. On the bridge the lyric strings together a sequence of Holly titles. Spencer sings it in an imitation of Holly's hiccuping style. The lead guitar break sounds like it is Kirwan.

EARL GRAY
(Kirwan)

KIRWAN'S instrumental, with its combining guitar lines and slightly unpredictable chord changes, is the only track on the album that comes anywhere near emulating the Peter Green period instrumentals. The piano line gives the tune a touch of dignity. The drums are mixed to one side and sound somewhat muffled. There's a fine moment where the drums drop out and the guitars are swathed in loads of reverb. The main weakness

of the track is the lack of a strong melody. It's a bit stiff.

ONE TOGETHER
(Spencer)

ACOUSTIC guitars start this gentle-paced song which takes on a country feel as soon as Spencer starts singing. The opening few seconds and the block harmony are two ingredients which would later be a part of the classic Mac sound of *Rumours*. Fleetwood plays the drums in a soft subdued manner and stays off the snare. There's a slide guitar and an easy-listening feel. Overall the track is mediocre, if pleasant ear-candy.

TELL ME ALL THE THINGS YOU DO
(Kirwan/Spencer/J. McVie)

AT LAST, a good track. A dirty boogie guitar sound starts off this number. This is probably the best track on the album with its doubled guitar riffs and attention to production. The first guitar solo is swathed in reverb and located in the distance. There's a funky electric piano and what sounds like a wah-wah guitar on one side. If only Paul Weller or Ocean Colour Scene could have made their 1996 recordings sound like this. There are nice splashes of cymbal over the top and a Hendrix-inspired guitar break in the middle. Great stuff.

Fleetwood Mac become a quintet in 1968, left to right: Mick Fleetwood, Peter Green, John McVie, Danny Kirwan and Jeremy Spencer.
(*Harry Goodwin*)

Peter Green's Fleetwood Mac
(February, 1968)

Fleetwood Mac in 1969, left to right: McVie, Green, Spencer, Kirwan and Fleetwood. (*Harry Goodwin*)

Mr. Wonderful (August, 1968)

The 1968-70 band relaxing in a dressing room. (*LFI*)

Then Play On (1969)

Peter Green. *(LFI)*

Kiln House (1970)

Christine Perfect joins the band, left to right: Mick Fleetwood,
Danny Kirwan, Jeremy Spencer, Christine and John McVie. *(LFI)*

Christine Perfect, Danny Kirwan, Mick Fleetwood, John McVie and Jeremy Spencer. *(Harry Goodwin)*

The 1972-74 band: Danny Kirwan, Bob Welch, Mick Fleetwood, Christine McVie and John McVie. *(LFI)*

Future Games (1971)

Bare Trees (1972)

Fleetwood Mac (1975)

The multi-million selling 1975 Fleetwood Mac, left to right:
Stevie Nicks, John McVie, Mick Fleetwood, Christine McVie
and Lindsey Buckingham. *(LFI)*

Celebrating the extraordinary success of their late-Seventies
renaissance, left to right: John McVie, Fleetwood,
Christine McVie, Buckingham and Nicks. *(LFI)*

Lindsay Buckingham. *(LFI)*

Stevie Nicks. *(LFI)*

Buckingham and Nicks on stage. *(LFI)*

MISSION BELL
(Kirwan)

BELLS INDEED feature on this track, which squanders a lovely opening when Spencer starts singing and throws the track back to the Fifties. It could be Billy Fury with a sentimental production. Christine McVie can be heard in the backing vocals. A disappointing end to a disappointing album.

The Original Fleetwood Mac

UK CBS 63875 May 1971; US Sire SR 6045 November 1977; reissue: UK Castle Communications ESSLP 026, ESSCD 026 (1990)

WHILE THE WORLD LISTENED TO *KILN HOUSE* AND WONDERED WHERE Fleetwood Mac would go next, the band's record label decided there were enough unreleased tracks in the archive to make up this collection. It's interesting, if unspectacular, harking back to the band's blues roots rather than the colourful musical excursions of *Then Play On*, so no hidden gems.

This album has been reissued on the Original Masters label (2000) with four extra tracks: 'Mighty Cold', 'Jumping At Shadows' [live], 'Somebody's Gonna Get Their Head Kicked In Tonight' and 'Man of Action'.

DRIFTING
(P.A. Green)

A SLOW 12-bar with a guitar/bass unison riff and some aggressive guitar on the intro that is moving toward Jimmy Page territory, though Green tends to play shorter phrases than Page. 'Drifting' has a sharp, vibrant production. Lyrically, it's a song in the My-Woman-Dun-Left-Me camp, though there's only one vocal verse before Green takes a fast solo.

LEAVING TOWN BLUES
(P.A. Green)

A LIGHTER blues with just guitar, bass and drums, and the guitar and voice shadowing each other. It has a slight country feel. The lyrics deal with the theme of leaving town, not returning, and going to Chicago. Which could be tricky if you live in Essex.

WATCH OUT
(P.A. Green)

AN UPTEMPO blues with a propulsive walking bass line and drums, and Green soloing in best bluesbreakers style before the first verse. The later guitar break features a brief slice of echo just to make things more interesting. Green mixes his scales in best style, frequently changing pickup to get different tones from his Les Paul. This song was also played during the *Blues Jam At Chess* sessions.

A FOOL NO MORE
(P.A. Green)

THIS IS A B flat minor blues with the trio, and a dry vocal pushed to one side of the mix. We're reading from the My-Woman-Dun-Mistreated-Me chapter of the Blues Lyric book. There's a terrific outburst of guitar after the first minute and again in the central solo, supported by authentic off-mike mumbles from Green. Typically, half-way through the solo, he winds down the volume. The last verse features another dramatic guitar burst before the subdued ending.

MEAN OLD FIREMAN
(Trad., Arr. Spencer)

THIS HAS Spencer singing on one side and an open-tuned acoustic playing slide on the other. You might cross-refer to Led Zep's 'Hats Off To (Roy) Harper'. This is probably one of Spencer's best recorded bits of playing, sounding quite authentic both in the way the bars are sometimes stretched and in its irregularity. His vocal is also free of mannerisms.

CAN'T AFFORD TO DO IT
(Williamson)

THIS IS AN uptempo blues featuring Spencer on vocals, distantly echoed by the others on the hook line. After a verse he takes a slide solo. Amazingly, he manages to avoid the Elmore James riff on this one. As the title indicates, the lyric tells of how he can't afford to lose his girl.

FLEETWOOD MAC
(P.A. Green)

GREEN USES a wonderful muddy raw tone for this 12-bar which is based on a pentatonic riff being played with the bass guitar while Fleetwood hits out a more intricate rhythm on the drums. There's a harmonica break but no second guitar. Green plays some interesting runs after the harmonica solo, changing to the neck pickup on the Les Paul toward the end for a rounded bell-like tone that was *de rigueur* for blues at the time. The number that gave the band their name, and one of the best tracks on the record.

WORRIED DREAM
(King)

A SLOW G minor blues with the rhythm section and piano supporting Green's authentic-sounding vocal. Green doesn't play any guitar until the end of the first verse. In the second verse he adds a few more phrases. The lyrics concern a dream in which some other man has taken his place. It's a taut reflection of male insecurity. Eventually he takes a solo on the front-pickup of the Les Paul, using a plaintive less-is-more approach, holding notes, fading phrases into silence, in the usual understated poetry of his style, but only through one 12-bar sequence. Then there's another vocal verse before the end. Green is fond of the minor key blues. He told me it was a musical 'space' in which he felt safe.

LOVE THAT WOMAN
(Leake)

S PENCER takes the vocal lead on this extroverted happy blues, which is very much in the mould of Muddy Waters. Thumping drums and rollicking piano and a distant slide guitar. Subtle it ain't, but it's fun.

ALLOW ME ONE MORE SHOW
(Spencer)

S LIDE-ACOUSTIC guitar by Spencer (in open G), on which Spencer sings. This is a 13-bar blues with an inserted bar at bar nine delaying the approach of the last phrase. Very much a demo performance, this must have sounded quite authentic when it was released.

FIRST TRAIN HOME
(P.A. Green)

A FEW LIQUID notes lead into another short minor key blues with a minimal arrangement of guitar, bass and drums. Green intersperses lead notes among the vocal phrases, and does a good impersonation of a black blues voice in terms of phrasing. After one verse he takes a solo, followed by another vocal verse. The lyrics are little more than a repetition of the title. There are some nice flurries of notes in the last verse and a sweet ending.

RAMBLING PONY NO.2
(P.A. Green)

T HIS IS another version of the 'Rambling Pony', which featured on *The Pious Bird of Good Omen*. It starts with driving bass and drums, followed by guitar voice and harmonica playing the tune. At about three minutes it fades away.

Future Games

US Reprise RS 6465 November 1971; UK Reprise K 44153 September 1971;
reissue: US CD Reprise 6465 2; UK CD WEA 927458 2

IN FEBRUARY 1971, AFTER THE RELEASE OF *KILN HOUSE*, FLEETWOOD MAC WENT to the US. While in San Francisco, Spencer expressed fears about going to LA. He felt something bad was going to happen there. Shortly after checking into their motel, Spencer said he was going out to the shops. He never returned. After several days of desperate searching, he was traced to a house occupied by the Children of God sect. He said he had joined the cult of his own freewill and has apparently remained with them to this day. Thus the band lost the second of its original members. Peter Green was invited to step in for the remaining dates, though according to Mick Fleetwood, the sets then consisted of 'Black Magic Woman' and 90 minutes of jamming.

After the tour the band returned to England to decide what to do next. The lease on Kiln House had expired, so they bought a similar property nearby called Benifols. In the summer of 1971 Californian singer/guitarist Bob Welch (who had been recommended to the band by Judy Wong) went down to the house in Hampshire to meet and rehearse with Fleetwood Mac. He was aware that he was being scrutinized not so much for his guitar skills, but for his psychological stability. He recalls, "They were traumatized because they'd gone from being one of the most successful bands to having two of their front men leave within a few months of each other."

Fleetwood said of Welch, "We loved his personality. His musical roots were more R&B instead of blues and that was refreshing. We thought it would be an interesting blend." Welch could also offer the benefits of a more trained musical mind.

The band played dates in the UK, France, Ireland and Holland in the following months then, in trying circumstances, they ploughed manfully on to record *Future Games*, their fifth studio album, with Kirwan and Christine McVie mostly handling the songwriting chores. The departure of Spencer meant the departure of the country and rock'n'roll pastiches that had detracted from *Kiln House*, and the Elmore James fixation which had been something of a stranglehold on the band's muse since its inception. Faced with the decision of where to go next, the Mac opted for a music dominated by more instrumental passages. The result of this is that at times they start to sound like Wishbone Ash. The vocals often take a back seat to the instrumental breaks. These songs very often do not have hooks and need editing down. 'Sands Of Time' is probably the stand-out number.

Fleetwood recalled, "We needed fresh material badly, plus a new identity and direction. We didn't want to be a purist blues group or an acid-rock band any more."

Welch remembers, "I had some songs that fit and they liked them enough to put them on the album. There was no producer, it was up to mutual consensus among Fleetwood Mac to make decisions. Basically Chris had to like it, then Mick. Danny meanwhile would disappear for days into the attic and eventually come down with a song. He was one of the strangest people I've ever met, very nervous, couldn't look you in the eye, hard to establish a rapport with. But he was also a very intuitive musician and at the age of twenty he played with a surprising maturity and soulfulness. There was an idealistic and pure thing about him that was great."

The sleeve photo was by Mick's sister Sally, showing her children Kells and Tiffany playing in the river Nadden near Salisbury. McVie had his shot on the back cover replaced by that of a penguin which in time would become an important symbol for the band. Its origins stem from a period when he and Christine lived near London Zoo where the resident penguins proved eternally fascinating to McVie.

WOMAN OF 1000 YEARS
(Kirwan)

STRUMMED, layered acoustic guitars start this track, whose verses slide down an unusual chord sequence. There are two male voices singing harmony throughout, and percussion is limited to congas and clave. Echo and reverb are used to give this song a spacey, drifting feel. The lead work on it lacks the character of earlier Fleetwood Mac. Lyrically, it seems suggestive yet unfocused, but with a nice title! It shows an advance in Kirwan's songwriting. The gentle laid-back vibe keeps the song dynamically on one level throughout. Consequently, it's perhaps over-long.

MORNING RAIN
(C. McVie)

STRIKINGLY less echoey than the previous track, 'Morning Rain' has a full mix with twin guitar harmony guitars jostling for space with the keyboards and rhythm section. Christine McVie can be heard sharing the lead vocal with one of the guys on this. You'll hear touches of wah-wah guitar on various parts. There's a distorted lead guitar break that answers the vocal lines. It rocks along in a fairly undistinguished manner. There's a hint of the later Seventies Fleetwood Mac – but only a small one. The long instrumentals show the song's weakness: the melody of the voices is second-best to the instrumental bits. Again, too long (this 42-minute album is compromised of only eight tracks) and fades out inconsequentially.

WHAT A SHAME
(R. Welch)

THE ALBUM'S shortest track is an instrumental that fades in and settles onto a heavy and slightly funky riff played by guitars, electric piano and honking bass saxes. Half way through, a sax takes a solo break while the band continue with the riff. This has all the hallmarks of a piece edited from some band jamming while they had a tape running. It stays on the one chord and fades away.

FUTURE GAMES
(R. Welch)

THE TITLE track is another epic at just over eight minutes. Reverbed high guitar chords recall Peter Green in a rippling effect before the drums enter with a thump. There's a short guitar break, then a gentle minor key verse, presumably sung by Welch, reflecting on the fate of lovers and what they did last night. By a stroke of early Seventies mixing, all the voices are over to one side. Christine McVie joins the tune toward the end of the verse. The chorus is a two-chord change with falsetto harmonies and a distant organ giving a slightly gospel feel to it. This is the most arresting moment on the album so far, but 'Future Games' is too long. At just under the third minute the intro of rippling guitar is reprised, followed by a short solo in the centre of the mix which becomes harmonised as it follows the melody. Though it's not easy to follow the lyrics, one of the themes which emerges is that you invent the future that you want to face. The falsetto voices on the chorus are reminiscent of Neil Young. Toward the six-minute mark there are some guitar phrases that wander around in the stereo image from side to side. If you're into that sort of thing, listen to this with headphones. Well-intentioned but rambling.

SANDS OF TIME
(Kirwan)

ANOTHER track that fades in and goes straight into a verse, with Kirwan singing about black nights, going down to the sea and the sands of time falling. When a chirruping lead guitar comes in over the delicate electric backing this could easily be the soft-rock of Wishbone Ash. That impression is strengthened toward the end when there's another guitar break using parallel thirds which gives way to sixths played by two guitars panned far left and right. The guitar break has two guitars keening against each other with the use of a volume pedal. The coda employs a similar idea. A slightly melancholy song despite the upbeat tempo and drumming. Minor chords predominate (it's in E minor). Again, there is a tendency for the vocals to give way to the instrumental sequences. In the middle you can hear electric piano passages. One of the stronger tracks, even at 7:35, 'Sands Of Time' shows maturity over Kirwan's earlier compositions.

SOMETIMES
(Kirwan)

DETUNED 12-string and piano lead this gentle rock number with garnishes of slide guitar over the top. It may remind you of 'Octopus' Garden' or something by Badfinger, and when you get to the chorus it could be CSN&Y. Kirwan takes the lead and harmonises with himself. He also sings a falsetto line far back in the mix with plenty of reverb. There's a nice burst of lead guitar. A song of missing love which is too long for the quality of the ideas.

LAY IT ALL DOWN
(R. Welch)

YES, I THINK we will. Starts with a heavy guitar riff and a slightly messed about time signature (5/4), and then settles into a funky minor chord riff for the verse. Welch's voice is doubletracked and has a touch

too much reverb, which makes it sound distant. The lyric talks about what's wrong with modern life and how the Bible might be right. Lay your burden down and enjoy paradise here on earth, says Welch. Hallelujah and pass the Marshall stacks. After the second chorus there's a long guitar solo which doesn't go anywhere over the monochord backing. This goes straight into the last verse. A rather dull song.

SHOW ME A SMILE
(C. McVie)

VERY DREAMY chords introduce this gentle ballad by Christine McVie, who weaves her melody over a chord sequence with a couple of surprises in it. Her voice is counterpointed by a high lead part with loads of reverb in the style of Green. The lyric seems to be sung to an unnamed child, reflecting her thoughts for the future. Although the melody is not as assured as it is in her later songs, there are a couple of flourishes on it which are very much her style. A pleasing song to conclude the album.

Bare Trees

US Reprise MS 2080 March 1972; UK Reprise K 44181,
released August 1972; reissue: US Reprise MSK 2278; US CD Reprise
2278 2; UK CD WEA Intl CD 2278 2

MOST OF **1972** WAS SPENT ON THE ROAD PROMOTING *FUTURE GAMES* IN THE US and Europe, opening for Deep Purple and Savoy Brown, but the period is also remembered for a tenseness in the relationship between Mr and Mrs McVie. *Bare Trees* was recorded during one week off in London. Unsurprisingly, it reflected tension, road fever and a longing for home. Disaster struck when the master mix was erased by airport security when they flew to New York. Several days were then spent re-mixing the album at the Record Plant. Sales were good in the US.

Kirwan wrote five of the tracks, but Bob Welch's 'Sentimental Lady', a US FM hit, is often regarded as the stand-out number. The quality of Kirwan's material had improved a bit, but the band were finding it less easy to get on with him. There was one track from Christine McVie that hinted at the type of song she would one day contribute to *Rumours*. There's still a tendency to sacrifice the songs to the instrumental passages but not quite as much as on *Kiln House*. *Bare Trees* came with a superbly atmospheric sleeve photo taken by John McVie.

CHILD OF MINE
(Kirwan)

THE ALBUM starts off with a fairly confident rock number sung by the writer. There are a few guitar licks in the distance, while a mix of guitars and keyboards glue it all together. Fleetwood gets to bash the cymbals a bit in this one. At the 1:30 mark you can hear congas over the electric piano. At one point Kirwan sings the same melody as the guitars are playing. Most of the lead guitars on this sound quite distant in the mix. It's another rambling guitar-dominated song, where the instrumental passages are more important than the sung parts. There's no obvious chorus or hook to focus proceedings. Christine McVie adds some backing vocals on the chorus. It's the longest track on the album. Somewhere in an alternate universe, Kirwan adds the word 'sweet' to the title, and makes Guns n' Roses redundant by 15 years. But sadly, not in ours.

THE GHOST
(R. Welch)

THIS LIGHTER song has what sounds like a Mellotron flute in it counterpointing the main vocal melody. Welch sings a tale of supernatural happenings on a slinky minor 7 backing that could be something by America or The Eagles. This is especially felt on the chorus where he provides a falsetto harmony with himself. 'The Ghost' has a stoned laid-back feel to it. This is a more commercially focused song than many of the others. Congas add a slightly funky touch to the acoustic sound. The instrumental parts are dominated by the flute rather than the guitar.

HOMEWARD BOUND
(C. McVie)

A CLASSIC cowbell 'Honky Tonk Women'-intro gets this one cranked, with piano and an electric guitar break. Christine sings this mid-tempo song of disillusionment with the whole life of touring, packing suitcases, and being on the road. As the descending chords of the chorus indicate, she is homeward bound. It's not one of her stronger melodies and there's an odd stiffness to her voice. The verse is constructed on a four-chord blues riff. It's noticeable that Fleetwood seems determined to drive the band a bit harder, with flurries on the kit and lots of four-to-the-bar snare. A few bars of harmonised guitar give way to a brief acoustic coda.

SUNNY SIDE OF HEAVEN
(D. Kirwan)

A N ETHEREAL atmosphere is established with this pleasingly melodic instrumental. A long descending scale figure goes over a romantic chord change, the net effect of which is to suggest the theme of 'You Only Live Twice'. This is one of Kirwan's best compositions, with the main guitar lead part climbing up various arpeggios. If this were dressed up a bit with a few more classical harmonies it could have been by Dutch band Focus. This is one of Fleetwood Mac's best post-Green tracks.

BARE TREES
(Kirwan)

T HE TITLE track is a more uptempo song that starts off with a one-chord groove with little flickers of soul guitar. A short verse with double-tracked vocals leads to a low single note riff which becomes the melody before going to the guitar break. There's a bit of scat singing with the guitar doubling, which comes across as very prog rock. It's not inspiring enough to be the title song and the music certainly doesn't in any way match the subtle atmosphere of John McVie's cover photography. There are at least four guitar tracks on this, moving into some guitar harmonies toward the end. The instrumental passages detract from the sung sections.

SENTIMENTAL LADY
(R. Welch)

THIS IS THE album's most celebrated track. Gentle piano and acoustic guitar start this love ballad, which is sung by Welch with a delightful backing vocal by Christine McVie. Welch comes up with another ballad which is commercial and shows up the contrast between his songwriting and the more instrumental numbers. The guitar solo features some queasy pitch-shifting from a rotary speaker or similar effects pedal. It has quite a strong melody. Watch out for the nice guitar lick on the fade.

DANNY'S CHANT
(Kirwan)

OR, 'A WAH-Wah Runs Through It'. Vicious wah-wah'd guitar creates a striking solo intro to this track which settles down to a mid tempo quite heavy rock tune in the mode of Cream. Kirwan's scat singing has loads of reverb on the voice, there are a few bits of slide guitar in the background, and Mick Fleetwood gets to do another quasi-African drum routine, leaving the snare out of the track's first couple of minutes. Although it doesn't have the requisite bite for this style, 'Danny's Chant' compels you to sit up and listen.

SPARE ME A LITTLE OF YOUR LOVE
(C. McVie)

MORE PICKETT-esque soul guitar on this intro. Christine takes the lead vocal addressed to her lover, and here she gets into her stride. This could have been covered by the later Fleetwood. Listen out for her distinctive trademark of bringing the tune down to the key note at the end of a phrase. The guitar solo seems to be played through a wah pedal that has been left back to emphasise lower frequencies and is slightly incongruous for the type of song. It has more of a verse/chorus structure than much of the album. The melody is a little stiff in parts and doesn't quite sit with the words in the last verse. The lyric has Christine placing herself in her pleading role. The coda is an increase of tempo that sends the song to the fade with a bit of a hoedown.

DUST
(Kirwan)

A PICKED electric guitar ushers in a quiet, reflective mood with a chord sequence that struggles to resist the pull of the E minor that started it. The chord sequence has some interesting twists in the minor chords. 'Dust' is concise, coming in under three minutes with no extended instrumental passages and a fairly abrupt ending.

THOUGHTS ON A GREY DAY
(Mrs Scarrot)

THE ALBUM'S bizarre 'Fortean' ending. Mrs Scarrot was a neighbour of the band near Benifols. She reads what might be a poem or a story, obviously recorded 'in the field', which mentions the bare trees of the album's title. It makes a strange end to the LP.

The sleeve note says "special thanks to Mrs Scarrot for her readings, recorded at her home in Hampshire". Makes you hope she lived long enough to enjoy some of the royalties.

Penguin

US Reprise Ms 2138 March 1973; UK Reprise K44235 May 1973; reissue: US CD Reprise 2138 2; UK CD Reprise 7599-26178-2

IN THE UK IN 1972, GLAM WAS RAPIDLY ECLIPSING PROGRESSIVE ROCK AND the charts were dominated by Slade, T.Rex and Ziggy-era David Bowie. Britain would clearly not be receptive to Fleetwood Mac, so to promote *Bare Trees*, they toured the US college circuit.

On tour Danny Kirwan's drinking had increased considerably and relations with him and the others were strained, with Mick Fleetwood ending up as the only member of the band talking to him. The crunch came before one gig when Kirwan smashed his vintage Les Paul Custom against a wall and refused to go on. They soldiered on that night, with Kirwan watching from the wings. After the gig, he offered some criticisms on how it could have been better! With reluctance, Fleetwood agreed with the others that Kirwan had to go and told him he was fired. Fleetwood Mac had now lost all three of their original guitarists.

In came Savoy Brown's vocalist Dave Walker and Long John Baldry's sideman Bob Weston. Fleetwood explained that Walker "was a bid for the big-time rock/boogie scene, alligator boots and the raised fist in the air", but there were some misgivings about him from the beginning. Bob Welch and Chris both thought he was too blatant, too rough around the edges and shallow as a performer. Fleetwood felt he was "an interpreter, not an original". Walker felt that the band wanted to get a bit more rock'n'rollish but thought he didn't do enough to justify being in it. They rehearsed the 7th line-up for a month before heading to Europe and then the US in the autumn and winter of 1972.

Penguin, named after John McVie's pre-occupation with the bird, suffered again from that habitual problem, a lack of musical focus. This was exacerbated both by the ghostly presence of the band's Green-era musical past and by Weston and Welch feeling from time to time that there was a palpable distance between them and the founding members.

There were simply too many styles. It seemed as if Fleetwood Mac were determined to produce their own sampler. Still struggling to find an identity, their experiments produced a wildly uneven collection of songs. Peter Green plays guitar on one track, 'Night Watch'.

REMEMBER ME
(C. McVie)

THE ALBUM starts with a bright and breezy uptempo rock number, with Christine double-tracking her vocal and occasional interjections by her own backing vocals. The melody throughout is counterpointed by Bob Weston's lead slide guitar. Listen for the little burst of harmonics in the main slide solo which, as a whole, doesn't quite justify its space. Lyrically, this is standard McVie territory. She needs him and you'd better believe it. It's time he remembered her. This is quite close to the later Fleetwood Mac, with Fleetwood steady throughout and John McVie providing a suitably melodic bass.

BRIGHT FIRE
(R. Welch)

THIS BEGINS with ambient sliding guitar chords over a distant organ backing and a flute-like melody. It then settles down into a slow groove with light drumming and an unusually mobile bass line from John McVie, who is the star of

the show. Bob Welch's murmured vocal and the major sevenths give the song a soft-focus jazz feel. You end up waiting for the flute break. It's that kinda tune.

Toward the end Christine supplies the only moment of drama with a high backing vocal cry.

DISSATISFIED
(C. McVie)

WITH A sudden punch, 'Dissatisfied' commences in the same vein as 'Remember Me', but with a stronger chorus. It kicks along at a medium tempo in a light-rock vein. There's a guitar break with a thin guitar tone and a side-dish of country bends, while Christine audibly double-tracks her voice (rather than using Automatic Double Tracking). It fades away fairly innocuously.

(I'M A) ROADRUNNER
(Holland/Dozier/Holland)

OR, BANDS Rush In Where Angels Fear To Tread. It's been suggested that this is the worst recording Fleetwood Mac ever committed to tape. I think that's a bit harsh, but here the Macs bite off rather more than they can chew. It's tight enough but can't be anything more than a pale imitation of Junior Walker's Motown 1965 original with harmonica replacing the honkin' sax. Dave Walker's vocal attempts to be black and gritty. He was apparently down the pub when he heard the band wanted to do this. As an attempt at a faithful rendition, it invites invidious criticism but I'm sure they had a ball recording it.

THE DERELICT
(D. Walker)

HARMONICA, acoustic guitars and a plucked banjo take us into folk-rock territory. You half expect Dylan to come in, but actually you get Bob Weston on vocals. This will probably remind you of The Band. Another example of Fleetwood Mac's musical identity crisis. It's only an average song, and also rather short, and would have needed a truly great singer to deliver a vocal to lift it.

REVELATION
(R. Welch)

ANOTHER switch of musical geography, this is a fast shuffling Santana-groove in a minor key with Welch singing and Weston supplying lots of lead guitar in a Santana style, especially toward the end. The

electric rhythm guitars are phased, and Fleetwood does a bit of African-style drumming. At almost five minutes it's too long, though there is a nice arpeggio passage starting with a lush major 7th chord. John McVie gets to come centre-stage with a short and effective bass break.

'Revelation' has an interesting lyric to fit the general vibe. Inevitably, this will draw comparison with some of Peter Green's Fleetwood Mac numbers.

DID YOU EVER LOVE ME
(C. McVie/R. Welch)

THIS GENTLY lilting song has the added interest of steel drums (played by Steve Nye) throughout to add an exotic Caribbean flavour. The first vocal phrases are shared between McVie and Weston, as is the chorus. The melody has a pleasing inevitability, which Christine's vocal brings out successfully. The lyric is a mature posing of a question about a love relationship. This is one of the album's best tracks.

NIGHT WATCH
(R. Welch)

A BIG HAND for Mr Peter Green (Slight Return) though you'll have to listen closely to catch him. The album's marathon at 6:09, 'Night Watch' starts with chord flourishes and a burst of Eagles-ish harmonised lead guitars. After the initial modest drama, the verse settles into a slow-ish reflective number, with Welch singing in that West Coast Joe Walsh mode. On the chorus he brings in some high block harmonies which make it sound like a track by America, who of course are the missing link between CSN&Y and The Eagles.

The middle guitar break by Green positions the main lead guitar in the back of the mix, with loads of reverb, doomy piano bass notes, quiet vocals and some strange drums from Fleetwood. Then, with a 'zing!' noise, the guitar solo returns and the track gets bogged down in repetition of an ascending chord sequence. A bit of a meandering track that doesn't fulfil its ambition.

CAUGHT IN THE RAIN
(B. Weston)

BOB WESTON's only cut on the LP fades in with dreamy wordless vocals, acoustic guitar and piano, and proceeds without vocals, though initially you'll live in fear that someone will start a spoken monologue about Jesus. They don't, the collection box is not passed round, and with a couple of folky hammer-ons the acoustic guitar brings things to a neat ending and an early bath.

Mystery To Me

US Reprise Ms 2158 October 1973; UK Reprise K44248 January 1974; reissued US Reprise Msk 2279; US CD Reprise 9 25982; UK CD Reprise 7599-25982-2

SHORTLY BEFORE THIS ALBUM WAS RECORDED THE BAND PARTED COMPANY with Dave Walker. The second album from the post-Sixties Fleetwood Mac was a collection of shorter pop material with a cover of 'For Your Love' by Graham Gouldman (by now enjoying hits with 10cc). The band were moving away from the slight flirtation with progressive rock and had long since left the blues. Mick Fleetwood thought very highly of the record and stated, "We all knew that *Mystery To Me* could have been a monster had we been able to properly go out and play behind it." In fact it ushered in the most fraught period in the band's whole troubled history. Fleetwood Mac would soon be fighting for their very identity.

On the cover of this album a tearful gorilla samples the delights of a cake on a beach. What did it mean? It's a mystery to me.

EMERALD EYES
(R. Welch)

A SLOW, heavily accented minor chord progression kicks off this record along with a few snatches of lead guitar over to one side of the mix. The chorus has some close harmony with Christine joining Welch on the lead. This has quite an American feel. After each chorus Weston takes a solo guitar break but none of them are especially memorable. This song, which is only an average opener, is mostly carried by the organ and piano.

The lyric concerns his lady with the emerald eyes who is still a mystery to him – alluding to the title of the LP. Did she look like a gorilla?

BELIEVE ME
(C. McVie)

A FEW DISTANT piano chords give way to a sprinkle of chords as Christine McVie starts what sounds like a ballad. Then, with a sudden switch of dynamics, the track rockets off at a frantic pace with a sort of speeded up Motown chord sequence and Christine harmonising with herself on the chorus. There's a brief guitar break with a nice touch of reverb on the drums, and then a slide guitar solo played by Bob Weston. The lyric is too vague and devoid of memorable images to stick in the mind or offer much of a hook. The drum sound gets noticeably more reverb-laden

towards the end, where a brief passage of harmonised guitar looks back to the band's illustrious past.

This track features some fluent piano work from Christine McVie.

JUST CRAZY LOVE
(C. McVie)

L YRICALLY, this is Christine McVie putting herself in her I'll-do-any-thing-for-you mode and as on her previous number, the lyric here doesn't offer any memorable details. This is another medium-paced rocker with some pleasing chord changes and guitar flurries, and the vocal, double-tracked, harmonised with itself, and very much to the front of the mix. The guitars provide a kind of counter-point melody. An average pop tune with only Christine's voice to lift it from being middle-of-the-road.

HYPNOTIZED
(R. Welch)

A TRIPLE time rhythm by Fleetwood brings this reflective ballad skittering in on the hi-hat. The arrangement features nice touches of acoustic guitar, electric piano and some jazzy fourths on the guitar. Welch's vocal may remind you of Sting who could have covered this, but was probably marking school essays in Newcastle at the time. The lyric has Welch musing about various landscapes including Mexico and New

Carolina. Weston takes a jazzy solo in the middle with loads of octaves while Welch hums against it. It's an unusual minor key groove which immediately stands out from the rest of the album. Christine McVie adds her voice to proceedings on some of the later choruses.

This was originally going to be something of a screamer for Dave Walker to get his alligator boots into. Welch recalls that it was influenced by the general atmosphere at Benifols, which was "rather spooky and strange, even in the summertime. There was an odd, ethereal mood around those grounds all the time, and a feeling that anything could happen."

FOREVER
(R. Weston/J. McVie/R. Welch)

THIS TRACK starts off in an almost Jamaican vibe with what sounds like a very early drum machine overlaid by live percussion, a prominent John McVie bass line and steel-drum touches. The guitar and the piano parts are both kept fairly thin so as to allow the arrangement to retain its light lilt, an effect which gives the track a reggae-like feel. This is a song about wanting to stay and enjoy the moment.

KEEP ON GOING
(R. Welch)

THESE imaginative titles just keep on coming. Not. Lyrically, an uneasy love song about living on borrowed time. A few dramatic minor chords on acoustic lead into this medium-tempo track, on which Christine McVie takes the initial vocal. This has a slightly soulful shuffle feel, with congas, sudden flourishes of strings, acoustic guitars and John McVie cutting loose a bit on bass. The main hook features quite an unusual descending chord pattern.

Like 'Hypnotized', this track manages not to be entirely predictable until you get to the mock-Spanish guitar break in the middle, which may have been played by Martin Birch, the producer, who has an acoustic guitar credit.

THE CITY
(R. Welch)

WELCH feels that New York is not a good place to be and berates it with this light rock track using what sounds like the tube-in-mouth-gizmo popularised by Peter Frampton. This is based on a 12-bar derivative and has all the bluesy guitar licks you would expect; the rollicking piano; and the tube gizmo making noises in the background. It takes a 12-bar solo in the middle. It's fairly ordinary. Just add water and dilute to taste.

MILES AWAY
(R. Welch)

THIS HAS a couple of witty references in the lyric to Andy Warhol, Don Juan (from the books of Carlos Castenada) and Hare Krishna; and another to the album title,"the mystery that there used to be".This is, perhaps, a song of disillusionment with certain hippie icons. After a medium tempo intro Fleetwood ups the ante by driving the song along while the guitars chatter to each other. Christine McVie can be heard singing on the descending chorus while Welch half sings and half speaks the verse. John McVie is obviously enjoying himself on bass. At one point the track thins out to a solo guitar with drums and bass and a blast of feedback. Gold star and a tick to the rhythm section for their performance here.

SOMEBODY
(R. Welch)

A LIGHT guitar riff with some 7th chords kick this off, then a rattlesnake percussion effect is panned from one side to another. Welch's voice is phased, making it sound smoky and slurry. The riffs wander and don't sound punchy. This is in the rock/soul groove of much of Hendrix's 1970 material, though not as imaginative or as well played as far as the guitar is concerned. Not an engaging track.

THE WAY I FEEL
(C. McVie)

PIANO and lilting acoustic guitar start this ballad in which Christine sings of making a fool of herself because she loves this guy and she can't hide it. It's probably her strongest tune on the album, showing the simplicity that will shine through in her later Seventies songs with the Nicks/Buckingham line-up.Very nice and compact.

FOR YOUR LOVE
(G. Gouldman)

YEP, THAT 'For Your Love'. This was a hit for The Yardbirds back in 1965 in their (for the time) exotic arrangement, and it allegedly precipitated Eric Clapton's departure from the band. Graham Gouldman was later to find fame as part of the UK hit-making group 10cc. Mac's version uses a fairly heavy beat through the first verse, suspending the famous four-chord sequence over a single bass note. They play the second section in a similar tempo, then develop the song by adding several bars and a twin-guitar break. It lacks the spooky baroque keyboard of the original. It's also longer. You may think this is a good thing, or you may not. It replaced an original number, 'Good Things'.

WHY
(C. McVie)

THE ALBUM closes with one of the longest tracks on it. This is a sad song of love gone wrong. The singer looks to the future knowing that she won't always feel this bad, but for the moment there is a hurt that won't go away

The solo slide guitar which starts 'Why' is followed by an acoustic guitar, piano, organ and strings, which combine to form a melodic cushion for Christine's voice. There are some nice, high, slide guitar notes. If U2 are watching, hey guys, cover this.

At the conclusion the main body of the sound dies away, leaving just two electric guitars and the strings. There's a sense of command about this track which makes it one of the best on the album, and an appropriate final shot.

Heroes Are Hard To Find

US Reprise MS 2196; UK Reprise K 54026, released September 1974; reissue: US CD Reprise 2196 2; UK CD WEA Intl 2196 2

AFTER THE RELEASE OF *MYSTERY TO ME*, THE BAND HIT THE ROAD IN THE FALL of 1973 but relations became further strained when toward the end of this tour Mick Fleetwood discovered that his wife had been having an affair with Bob Weston. The band continued with the tour for a while, but the atmosphere soon became unbearable.

On October 26, 1973, the band met to discuss the situation, and Bob Weston was sacked. They told manager Clifford Davis they needed a few weeks to re-group before they could play any more concerts. He was angry and accused them of being irresponsible. A short while later the band discovered that Davis had put together another group called Fleetwood Mac, and had sent them off on a ten-week tour of the US. Davis was to claim in subsequent litigation that he owned the rights to the name. The fake Fleetwood Mac were immediately rumbled by audiences and given a rough-ride, but their activities did absolutely nothing to further the careers of the real Fleetwood Mac, whose legal battle with Davis would last for five years.

A fateful decision was made to leave England and settle in California. Christine McVie was reluctant to go but was persuaded to try it for six months. Fleetwood Mac arrived in the US in the spring of 1974 with no management and hardly any money, once more down to a quartet. With the support of impresario Bill Graham, the band got Warner Bros to let them record a new album, *Heroes Are Hard To Find* and then went on tour to promote it. They played about 43 shows, made little money but repaired some of the damage caused by their impersonators. By the end of this tour, Bob Welch had decided that he needed a break and left to pursue a solo career.

Christine McVie and Bob Welch wrote all the songs on *Heroes Are Hard To Find*, an album which is even weaker than its predecessor, due in part to Welch's rather introspective musical taste and dated songwriting style.

This is the last album of Fleetwood Mac's wilderness years between the departure of Peter Green and the arrival of Stevie Nicks and Lindsey Buckingham.

HEROES ARE HARD TO FIND
(C. McVie)

CHRISTINE'S voice starts the album off over a slightly monotonous two-chord groove with touches of brass. This is followed by a descending chord sequence hook. There is only one short instrumental passage here, apart from which the focus is resolutely on the song. Lyrically, it's not quite clear whether she's saying you should make the best of your lover because heroes are hard to find or get rid of him anyway and be patient. This was released as a single, but didn't make much of a ripple.

COMING HOME
(Welch)

HERE WE get a subdued intro with phased guitars in the distance, strings and a spoken passage. There are echoed keyboards and a siren-like voice. A lead guitar comes in with an octave melody, while John McVie plays one of his busiest bass lines. Eventually Welch comes in with a stoned vocal laid back over the busy rhythm section, which creates an odd feeling of tension. 'Coming Home' is a strange track which, like some other things by Welch, is vaguely reminiscent of The Police. It makes quite a contrast with the opening track, indicating that the band still hadn't really got a strong sense of their musical direction.

ANGEL
(Welch)

THIS FADES in on a slowish minor chord change with competing guitar lines. A sluggish rhythm is established before Welch, without much warning, starts the verse. There are slight musical references to The Eagles and The Doobie Brothers. The arrangement is quite full but places a number of the instruments in the distance. 'Angel' is the key-word for the chorus, which has no melody to speak of.

BERMUDA TRIANGLE
(Welch)

SUBDUED drums and a sustained synth patch with some ornate guitar provide the backing as Welch sings about the famous Bermuda Triangle, the 'black hole' into which ships and planes (and perhaps The Osmonds!) purportedly disappear. After a minute it picks up into a stronger driving rhythm, but there is no real melodic interest. When the guitar break comes, it's on the acoustic. This is monotonous and never lives up to the potential interest of its lyric theme.

COME A LITTLE BIT CLOSER
(C. McVie)

BUT WE hardly know you... Oh, alright. This features pedal steel guitar played by 'Sneaky' Pete Kleinow who adds a nice solo break in the middle. Starting with just piano, the song gets going when the rhythm section comes in with a bash. As it proceeds, we get some George Harrison-style high slide guitar over the strings and guitars. Christine's voice is becoming more confident and the melody has her hallmark turns, just as the lyric comes squarely from her pleading lover persona. The arrangement needs to be clarified, but otherwise this is getting close to the classic Mac sound of the mid-Seventies.

SHE'S CHANGING ME
(Welch)

A MEDIUM pop number with a touch of volume-swell guitar for the intro. This is a guitar effect in which the note is played with the volume of the guitar down and then (either by a footpedal or by manipulating the volume control on the instrument) is turned up, so the note gets louder after it is struck. The song has quite an Eagles feel, with the block harmonies throughout the verse. The overall sound is commercial and fairly bland. The lyric is a piece of woman-worship typical of the genre. A rather lightweight track.

BAD LOSER
(C. McVie)

FLEETWOOD starts this minor key tune with one of his African jungle rhythms, with lush guitars in the background. The rhythm is a sort of bastardised samba. Christine takes the lead, though her melody doesn't seem to sit very well with the arrangement. There's a couple of touches of guitar high chords swathed in reverb which recall Green-era Mac. One of those tracks where the instrumental side becomes more significant than the vocal. Overall, not a very successful song.

SILVER HEELS
(Welch)

"SHE CAME in like a hurricane," sings Welch, which doesn't quite set up this track. He gets in references to *The Blackboard Jungle*, Paul McCartney and Etta James. Welch's lyrics tend to be more interesting than Christine McVie's. Musically, this has a stronger melody than some of his other songs, but there's something stilted about it. There are a few touches of harmonised guitars and audible phasing on McVie's bass, but overall, this is an average number.

PROVE YOUR LOVE
(C. McVie)

A SLOW tempo ballad with McVie singing wordlessly with the piano on the intro. This has a slinky feel. The melody has some distinctive jumps in it, and chords are displaced into unexpected positions. The solo break is taken by the electric piano. Strings are prominent in the background, as is a very forcefully strummed acoustic guitar on one side of the mix. Melodically, it's one of the stronger tracks on the album.

BORN ENCHANTER
(Welch)

COWBELL, vibes, piano trills, and a guitar being put through an octave splitter combine to make for an exotic intro to this groove number in which Welch tries to emulate a black feel. Soon the guitar, swathed in reverb, takes over the lead. Welch sounds like he's singing in falsetto. John McVie keeps most of the verse going with a two-note riff that runs persistently throughout. This is a daring arrangement with more space in it than the band usually gave at this time, but it doesn't quite manage to create the voodoo vibe it wants. The cross-reference here would be the vibe on Bob and Earl's 'Harlem Shuffle'.

SAFE HARBOUR
(Welch)

A SWIRLING guitar intro with cymbal rolls, side-drums and Welch's jazzy guitar octaves start this track in a pseudo 'Albatross' vein. The trouble with Welch's lead playing is that he throws notes and phrases away as though he's rehearsing for something, instead of playing them for keeps. This is more or less an instrumental track until the end, when Welch comes in with two vocal lines. Pleasant but not especially engaging.

Fleetwood Mac

US Reprise MS 2225 July 1975; UK Reprise K 54043 August 1975;
reissues: UK Limited Edition White Vinyl K 54043; US Reprise 2281;
US CD Reprise 2281 2 (1983); reissued as a double album with *Rumours*
Warners WEA MC K466103

WITH BOB WELCH GONE, FLEETWOOD MAC WERE DOWN TO THE TRIO OF
Mick, John and Christine. Mick Fleetwood, looking for a place to record
the band's next album, was in Sound City Studios in Los Angeles where he
heard a tape of a duo called Buckingham-Nicks. Stevie Nicks and Lindsey
Buckingham had been together in a band called Fritz which had supported
many of the famous names of the San Francisco area in the late Sixties. After
Fritz broke up, the two had decided to carry on and eventually released an
album in November 1973. Unfortunately, it didn't create much interest.

Mick Fleetwood made enquiries as to who they were and asked
Lindsey Buckingham to join Fleetwood Mac and make a quartet, but it soon
became clear that he wasn't joining without his partner Stevie Nicks. Thus
was formed the classic Seventies Fleetwood Mac line-up. Of joining the
band, Nicks once said, "Since I have a deep love for the mystical... I thought
this might be the band for me because they are mystical, they play
wonderful rock'n'roll, and there's another lady, so I'll have a pal."

Their tenth studio album was recorded by the new line-up in about 10
days at Sound City, Los Angeles. Christine McVie had 'Over My Head', 'Warm
Ways' and 'Sugar Daddy' on demo; Buckingham had 'Monday Morning' and
'I'm So Afraid'; Stevie Nicks had 'Landslide' and 'Rhiannon'; and 'Crystal' was
recast from the Buckingham-Nicks solo album.

Buckingham soon showed that he had strong ideas about production.
There were the usual crises – at one point the master tapes were lost and
put in a pile to be erased – but something about the material, the
performers and the time clicked, and the band began a rapid ascent to the
kind of success achieved by very few. FM radio picked up on the album –
indeed Fleetwood Mac and 'FM' became synonymous – and by Christmas
1975 *Fleetwood Mac* had sold a million and a half copies. It made number 1 in
the US in November 1976, and was double platinum by 1977. It yielded three
hit singles 'Over My Head', 'Rhiannon' and 'Say You Love Me', songs that went
on to figure in the band's live sets for many years. This was a grand new
beginning for the group. At last they had stepped out of the shadow of
Peter Green.

This is sometimes known as their *white album*, not to be confused
with that of a well-known Liverpool band.

A de-luxe version of the album (Reprise 8122-73881-2) was released in

March 2004 and contains the following extra tracks: 'Jam #2', 'Say You Love Me' [single version], 'Rhiannon (Will You Ever Win)' [single version], 'Over My Head' [single version] and 'Blue Letter' [single version].

MONDAY MORNING
(Buckingham)

THE NEW era dawned with this highly commercial medium tempo song. The verse, derived from a 12-bar pattern, is strongly accented. The key ingredients of the classic mid-Seventies Mac sound are established here: faultless timing, a strong melody with block harmonies on the chorus from Christine, Nicks and Buckingham, and Buckingham supplying a guitar solo for the middle eight which is kept short and to the point. The mood of the song is optimistic, despite its title.

WARM WAYS
(C. McVie)

THIS HAS A softer feel with electric piano, acoustic guitar, and spacey lead guitar, and Mick Fleetwood uses some of the tom-tom drumming touches that he used with Peter Green. The song has a rich descending chord sequence at the end of the verse and a romantic minor chord to round off the chorus. The melody is sung by Christine McVie in her best low timbre and with some distinct vocal inflections. Buckingham supplies some very sweet high slide guitar and

there are wordless backing harmonies. A subtle and pleasingly romantic number with the drums dropping out for the last few bars, Dusty Springfield ought to have covered this.

BLUE LETTER
(Curtis)

THE ALBUM'S only non-original song came about because the song's writers, the Curtis Brothers, were using the studio at the same time as Fleetwood Mac. Buckingham takes the lead vocal and is supported by the others — Nicks' harmony being very noticeable — over two distorted rhythm guitars and another guitar playing fills. This is good-time West Coast rock, the sort that radio stations loved. It rocked, but not too much. Buckingham takes a reasonably plangent solo in the middle but keeps it short. Rule number 34 of great pop: no noodling!

RHIANNON
(Nicks)

A STAND-OUT track on the album, this haunting song gave Nicks a larger-than-life persona on stage and hooked in plenty of impressionable young American girls who wore their hair long and liked to dress in long flowing skirts. It's a brilliant arrangement with the rhythm section staying off a straight rock beat, Buckingham supplying twin rising guitar parts either side of the mix, and a suggestion of electric piano. On the second chorus Buckingham adds some very tasteful fills in the spirit of Green. The title is sung in memorable block harmonies, resulting in a very effective hook. Lyrically, Nicks describes a *femme fatale* of the poetic variety, and the line about never having seen a woman taken by the wind appealed immensely to her female fans.

Live, this became an epics of their set, the band's very own 'Stairway To Heaven'. 'Rhiannon', of course, is a Welsh name, and Nicks often introduced it as "a song about a Welsh witch". What they thought of this in Merthyr or Swansea is unrecorded. This was a Top 20 single in the US and became one of the band's most famous songs.

OVER MY HEAD
(C. McVie)

FADING IN as a gentle groove on a major chord before shifting to a minor on a rumble of guitar and piano, this track features Christine McVie singing of a lover who is driving her nuts yet delighting her at the same time. The chorus features some nice harmony with herself. There is a distant organ at the back of the mix and several voices

singing the title and some odd touches of percussion. It has something of the same gentle quality as 'Warm Ways', and fades out quietly. The live version of this is more powerful, and therefore much better.

'Over My Head' deservedly went into the US Top 10 as a remixed single in November 1975. This was one of several songs Christine McVie wrote on a portable Hohner electric piano in an apartment overlooking the beach at Malibu.

CRYSTAL
(Nicks)

THIS SONG opens with Buckingham singing the first verse gently over the changes before the triple time is established over an Am-G-F sequence, supported by Nicks' vocals. The song has something of the breezy polish of The Eagles, but is prettier. After the second chorus, there is a brilliant moment of ascending bass under the high-pitched synth solo while the chords are moving in the opposite direction and this is still there as the song begins its slow fade. It says much for Buckingham's musical taste that he didn't insist on playing a guitar solo over this coda, or that the band didn't decide to have a more dramatic climax. The crystal of the title reflects the crystal knowledge of a lover.

SAY YOU LOVE ME
(McVie)

SIDE TWO of the vinyl album opens with the best Christine McVie song on the record, a swinging rocker featuring acoustic piano, banjo, and the usual harmonies on the chorus. It's a song of love lost and recovered, though there's a slightly bitter-sweet quality to it, a feeling that it could all go wrong again. The middle eight is wonderful, picking up that mood and featuring two Buckingham solos, the first chiming, the second more of an electric lead. On the coda of "falling, falling, falling", a chiming 12-string comes through loud and clear, and there's a fine bass line from McVie.

This was a Top 20 single in the US. Christine McVie recalls that it was one of the first songs that they ever rehearsed with Buckingham and Nicks: "I started playing 'Say You Love Me', and when I reached the chorus they started singing with me, and fell right into it. I heard this incredible sound – our three voices... I couldn't believe how great this three-voice harmony was."

A great live number with a very strong chorus.

LANDSLIDE
(Nicks)

THIS QUIET acoustic ballad is led by capoed acoustic guitars and features some very romantic imagery. The bittersweet nature of the song follows on well, and the image of disaster in the landslide anticipates the turmoil which will lead to *Rumours*. The last few bars before the first pause at the end have a nice build-up and there's a sudden ending. There are some interesting differences between this and the live version. Some of the melody goes into Nicks' lower register, and the high-drama of her later live performances make this version seem a little perfunctory. On stage, it became another song altogether, tailor-made for getting audiences eating out of the palm of her hand.

WORLD TURNING
(McVie/Buckingham)

THIS WAS written in the studio while Lindsey, Christine and Mick were jamming. Two acoustic guitars, one electric and Fleetwood's rattling hi-hat rhythm support this bluesy tune, which is sung by Buckingham. This is about as close as this line-up ever got to Peter Green's Fleetwood Mac. After two verses Fleetwood brings in his bass drum, and Buckingham sings some phrases with himself. Lyrically it's lightweight, a simple statement of confusion and feeling slighted by people. The gradual build throughout culminates in a short sequence with standard drums toward the end and the busy guitars quieting down to a bluesier rhythm and lead. There are even some 'talking' drums toward the close. Probably one of the less inspired tracks.

SUGAR DADDY
(McVie)

THIS NUMBER, another very catchy track sung by Christine, has a groove which is almost soul, and is led by piano, organ and a neat McVie bass line. Buckingham turns in another fine complementary solo. The attractive chromatic chord changes in the latter part of the verse recall the Stax groove of 'Sitting On The Dock Of The Bay'. The lyric compares her need for a sugar daddy who provides money and nice things, to her love for her man. One of the best tracks on the album.

I'M SO AFRAID
(Buckingham)

THE ALBUM ends with this doomy minor key number, which, judging by the rhythm section, was inspired by earlier Fleetwood Mac line-ups. Buckingham sings the first chorus falsetto, then there's a passage of harmonised guitar which is very Eagles and could easily have come from something like *Hotel California*. The lyrics are unable to come up with any memorable

images to support the atmosphere of the music. The playing shows how, as a lead guitarist, Buckingham understood the mileage that could be got out of staying on a single note or group of notes. This song had to wait for a concert performance before it could really blossom. The live version is much better because Buckingham sings it much more forcefully.

Rumours

US Warner Bros BSK 3010; UK Warner Bros K 56344,
released February 1977; Limited Edition White Vinyl Reprise (Import)
Warner Bros 56344; UK His Masters Voice C88 1-1 (limited edition box
set, 3500 copies with 12-page booklet);
US CD Warner Bros 3010 2 (1983); UK CD Warner Bros 256344 (1983)

OR, A CIRCUS, A NIGHTMARE, A MIRACLE. THE PRESSURE OF CONTINUOUS touring to support the quintet's first album created enormous personal stresses, the consequence of which was that the relationships within the band all seemed to be breaking while recording the follow-up. No-one was speaking to each other and life in the studio was very tense. Mick Fleetwood's wife Jenny (sister of Patti Boyd, who married George Harrison and then Eric Clapton) left California and returned to England. Nicks and Buckingham split, and Christine and John McVie had broken up on the road. This lent a somewhat bittersweet humour to the photos on the back sleeve which depict members of the band embracing as if no-one can remember who goes with whom. The front cover reprised the mysterious sphere from the last album and the quaint theatrical trappings. Stevie Nicks was now in full flight as the winsome California fairy in ballet shoes and drapes, the result of her 'Rhiannon' stage persona.

Producer Richard Dashut recalled, "The band brought some great songs with them, but they needed arrangements and a unified sound. All I can say is that it was trial-by-ordeal, and the craziest period of our lives. We went four or five weeks without sleep, doing a lot of drugs. I'm talking about cocaine in such quantities that at one point I thought I was really going insane. The whole atmosphere was really tense, with arguments all the time and people storming in and out. To relieve the tension we'd look for sexual release, but even that didn't help much... The only refuge was in the music... At one point, things got so tense between us all that I remember sleeping right under the soundboard one night because I felt it was the only safe place to be."

In his account of the band's history, Fleetwood says that "everyone made tremendous emotional sacrifices just to show up at the studio".

Recording took place at the Record Plant, in Sausalito, California and proceedings were apparently hampered by a number of unwelcome phenomena, including a tape machine that chewed up tapes, a piano that didn't want to be tuned even after four days (they tried nine pianos and eventually gave up on the idea), and a large number of sightseers who came over when word got out that Fleetwood Mac were recording there. The band would spend several days trying to get a drum-sound for one track. Away from Sausolito the tapes sounded horrible and the band ended up re-recording all the parts. A potentially lucrative spring tour in 1976 had to be cancelled (despite the success of the 'Rhiannon', which had been released as a single) because the album was not completed to the perfectionist requirements of the musicians. The band had 10 days' rehearsal in June for a summer tour and hit the road.

The album was recorded under the working title *Yesterday's Dreams*, but John McVie changed it to *Rumours*. It sold a million copies in the first month of release; went on to top 20 million sales; spent 31 consecutive weeks at number 1; and became one of the all-time best-selling albums ever. It spent an amazing 400 weeks in the UK Top 100. How does one explain such success?

Rumours had a commercial set of songs in a melodic soft-rock radio-friendly vein. It had guitar solos that never outstayed their welcome; 'unplugged' acoustic moments of crystal clarity; West Coast breezy harmonies in the grand Beach Boys/Mamas and Papas/Eagles tradition; and three distinctive strong lead voices. With a mix of male and female singers, the band could avoid drawing an audience biased towards one gender or the other. It was 12" of soap-opera: given the treatment of the relationship themes, there was something to which everyone could relate. *Rumours* was a cut diamond with a thousand facets. However you held it up to the light, a glint would catch your eye. And breaking up never sounded so musical.

One odd track from the sessions, Nicks' 'Silver Springs', was held over and put on the B-side of 'Go Your Own Way'.

A de-luxe version of the album (Warner Bros 8122-73882-2) was released in 2004 and contains the following extra tracks on a second CD divided into two parts, 'Roughs and out-takes' and 'Early Demos': 'Second Hand News', 'Dreams', 'Brushes (Never Going Back Again)', 'Don't Stop', 'Go Your Own Way', 'Songbird', 'Silver Springs', 'You Make Loving Fun', 'Gold Dust Woman #1', 'Oh Daddy', 'Think About It'; 'Never Going Back Again', 'Planets of the Universe', 'Butter Cookie (Keep Me There)', 'Gold Dust Woman', 'Doesn't Anything Last', [Jam sessions] 'Mic The Screecher', 'For Duster (The Blues)'.

Rumours is also available as a DVD-A with 'Silver Springs' included, and there is a DVD documentary about *Rumours* in the Classic Albums series (WEA/Rhino 1998).

SECOND HAND NEWS
(Buckingham)

R*UMOURS* kicks off with this jaunty acoustic-driven upbeat number in which Nicks supplies the backing vocal and Buckingham plays sprightly harmonics on an open-tuned guitar. The image of 'going down in the long grass' to 'let me do my stuff' struck an erotic chord and made it a great party record. There's almost a jugband quality to this. The title may have suggested that the singer was down and out but the mood was buoyant, and faded out on a few seconds of guitar lead. Short 'n' sweet.

DREAMS
(Nicks)

I*N WHICH* our Lindsey gains the coveted P. Green award for gallant guitar conduct. This is Buckingham's finest hour as a guitarist, using a volume pedal on his lead fills to produce a moody accompaniment to Nicks' tale of what happens to those who make decisions they regret. The whole track is based on a mere three chords climbing up and back. There's a hint of strings, strummed acoustic, and McVie is rock steady on bass throughout. The lyrics allude back to the crystal vision of 'Crystal' on the previous album, and the image of the players picks up the imagery of the theatre suggested by the sleeve. The essential ambi-

guity of the song lies in whether the singer is addressing herself in a mood of self-recrimination and weary wisdom or whether she is addressing someone else and suppressing a whole ocean of grief. The line about being washed clean by the rain which appears at the end was another of those universal motifs that appeal to everyone. Romantic disenchantment is the best disenchantment of all. 'Dreams' ends on a high string note and a chilling couple of notes from Buckingham. One of the few tracks by the later Mac that approach the intensity of the best of Peter Green, and successfully revived by Irish group The Corrs in 1998.

NEVER GOING BACK AGAIN
(Buckingham)

T*HIS IS A* brief acoustic interlude fingerpicked for a folk feel. The guitars are capoed high for additional brightness, with occasional vocal lines from Buckingham and a little vocal support from the others. Once more, the lyrics are enigmatic: what was it that he was never going back to again? Buckingham was able to make good capital out of this live.

DON'T STOP
(C. McVie)

P*IANO*, strings, and a gradual drum build-up establish an intense rocking dance track that can't fail to get the feet moving, and conveys an optimistic sentiment of looking forward to a better future. The vocal is shared between Christine and Lindsey who take a verse each and share the brilliantly catchy chorus. Buckingham turns in a neat economic solo in the middle just to spice things up. There are nice touches to the arrangement like the sudden stop toward the end; the repeated guitar note; and the occasional touches of honky-tonk piano. The coda fades on the advice "Don't you look back".

John McVie recalls, "I'd be sitting there in the studio while they were mixing 'Don't Stop', and I'd listen to the words which were mostly about me, and I'd get a lump in my throat. I'd turn around, and the writer's sitting right there."

'Don't Stop' received a second lease of life when it was adopted as a presidential campaign song for Bill Clinton's Democratic bid for the White House. The five members reunited to play the song live at Clinton's pre-Inauguration Ball in January 1993.

GO YOUR OWN WAY
(Buckingham)

THE TEMPO is sustained with this track, driven by a powerful drum rhythm during the verse. The chorus breaks into standard rock drumming and brings in the others for the harmony on the hook. There's some strong electric rhythm, and the mood see-saws between the promise of the verse – the singer offering her the whole world – and the chorus which expresses the pain of telling her to go her own way and suffer the consequence of another lonely day. Buckingham builds the coda's intensity through a neat guitar solo which slowly increases in pitch. It was obvious that this – probably the rockiest number on *Rumours* – would be a very strong number in the live set.

SONGBIRD
(C. McVie)

TO GET this exquisite take, the band took a mobile into an empty auditorium at Berkeley University. Fleetwood said, "It should sound like Christine is sitting alone at the piano after a concert, when everyone has gone home." That was exactly how it came out. The rock of the previous two songs gives way to this beautiful, plaintive track with piano and chorus. The lyrics are generous and melancholy. She sings to a departed lover, promising never to be cold, for love is both sharper and deeper even though the songbirds know the score – an effective use of a colloquial word in this context. There's an emotional simplicity and depth here, and the song is almost classically controlled in the way she decides to end the track without going for the obvious heart-wrenching twists. As a result it has dignity under pressure, and nothing of the fey romanticism which often weakens Nicks' songs. Christine's Perfect Hour.

THE CHAIN
(Buckingham/McVie/Nicks/ Fleetwood/McVie)

'THE CHAIN' was created by splicing tapes of several different bits of music together. This is the only fully collaborative effort on the album, starting with some bluesy guitar, a bass thump and distant harmonised vocals. When the first chorus comes in there's some lovely keyboard in the background and an effective vocal arrangement where the hook line is echoed first by Nicks and then much higher with reverb by McVie. The lyrics give open expression to hurt and pain in the "damn your love, damn your lies" lines. The sentiment is a powerful one. Once you said you would never break things up – but you did. There's a brief pause before McVie enters with a memorable bass riff that became famous in the UK in the Nineties when it was used as the theme for televised Formula One Grand Prix racing. Buckingham winds things up with a solo in the Neil Young mode of seeing how much mileage you can get out of a couple of notes. The band then bring in another harmony vocal hook. The lyric expresses the idea that the chain has become a way of linking lovers and is no bad thing but on a broader allegorical level it could refer to the unbroken chain of

circumstance that has held Fleetwood Mac together through thick and thin since their inception in 1967.

YOU MAKE LOVING FUN
(C. McVie)

A PHASED electric piano gives this track a funky feel despite the minor chord opening. Christine takes the vocal on a lyric that tells of fun, but the musical setting digs a bit deeper. The chorus features stunning vocal harmony arrangements, adding a ghostly back-up and some brilliant guitar work from Buckingham, who hits just the right notes quietly in the background of the verse and then comes in with a fine melodic solo after the first chorus. Equally great is his repeated guitar phrase at the back of the chorus. Christine's vocal on the last verse suggests she's trying to win back her man. The ending of the song is deeply plaintive with the massed harmonies in counterpointed with some extraordinary lead guitar by Buckingham, who shows a wonderful melodic ear here.

I DON'T WANT TO KNOW
(Nicks)

A COUSTIC guitars start off this dead-ringer-for-Cat-Stevens until the vocals come in, shared by Nicks and Buckingham. This is a simple, sprightly, uptempo, three-chord major song with handclaps and some nice touches and a simple tight bass line. It sounds more upbeat than the lyric probably suggests, though the general state is one of confusion. Buckingham comes up trumps again on the guitar solo, making use of the top string as a pedal note while the other note moves around.

OH DADDY
(C. McVie)

WRITTEN for Mick Fleetwood, the only father in the band, this opens very quietly with a synth flute sound and two acoustic guitars, before the doomy first piano chord. In a lyric that speaks of mistakes made and regretted, Christine admits that he's right and she's wrong. There are some stirring moments of sudden accented chords, John McVie's bass line moves around in a pleasing manner and there are nice guitar touches. The mood is not quite as naked as 'Songbird' but has instead a tone of self-criticism in a restrained performance and arrangement.

GOLD DUST WOMAN
(Nicks)

THERE'S A fade into this track with some strange throaty sitar-like sounds accompanying the acoustic guitars. It's another subtle arrangement, patient in the way in which it builds but it lacks the atmosphere of 'Rhiannon'. Nicks uses her fey rapid vibrato, and is joined by Christine McVie and Buckingham on the chorus harmony. The lyric seems to issue a warning, anticipating the feel of her solo material. At one point there's a patented banshee wail by Nicks, dropping down the notes, leading to the coda, which sees indulging her taste for the Gothic by singing about black widows. This was take eight of a long, arduous recording session one night and doesn't have the emotional or commercial appeal of some of the other tracks.

Tusk

US Warner Bros 3350 October 1979; UK Warner Bros K 66088;
US CD Warner Bros 2694 2 (1987); UK CD Warner Bros 266088 (1987)

1977 WAS MOSTLY SPENT TOURING OFF THE BACK OF RUMOURS METEORIC success. There were more in-band traumas, including Fleetwood and Nicks embarking on an affair. They swept the American Music Awards and early in 1978 resolved the litigation with Clifford Davis which had been hanging over them since 1974. They also had the 156th star on Hollywood's Walk of Fame.

For *Tusk*, the band invested almost one and a half million dollars in Studio D at the Village Recorders in LA. Lindsey Buckingham was acutely aware of the changes that had been going on in music over the past few years, in particular punk and the reaction against so-called dinosaur bands. Fleetwood Mac were targeted for a certain amount of derision on three accounts: first, over the style of music they played; second, because they were so successful; and third, because they were perceived (in the UK) as American. Buckingham wanted the new album to be a contemporary artistic statement.

Question: how do you follow-up a squillion-selling album that half the northern hemisphere seems to have bought? Answer: you make another one just like it? Wrong. You face the music and do something different. Lindsey Buckingham for one was hell-bent on not allowing *Tusk* to become *Rumours II: The Accountants Strike Back*. They opted to record a double album but there is a truism about double albums which states that in almost every case there is a much better single record waiting to get out. *Tusk* is no exception but its two discs were unable to supply as many singles as *Rumours*. However, it did sell five million copies, which is more than most bands could dream of.

Lindsey Buckingham dominated the project, writing half the songs and overseeing the production. It is said that tensions were increased in the band because he spent months working alone in the studio. Sales of the album weren't helped when the album was played on US radio in its entirety, thus ensuring that a million tape players were at the ready to copy the whole thing and save their owners the bother and expense of buying it. In addition, Warner thought the band crazy to release a double album of off-the-wall material. In 1979-80 the recording industry was in a slump which only Led Zeppelin with *In Through The Out Door* had really been able to overcome. Mick Fleetwood wanted the material to sound more like the band's classic stuff and the McVies were not happy about Lindsey's segregated way of working. It didn't help also that work on the album started in May 1978 and was interrupted by the *Penguin Country Summer Safari* tour in July and August.

It was certainly to their credit that Fleetwood Mac resisted recording *Rumours Part 2*, but their attempt to make a record that sounded different doesn't really work and gives the impression of a band stretching its talents too thinly. Some of the tracks have a throwaway feel about them, half-ideas that should've been left alone or pushed much further than they were. None of the band's songwriters are able to do much with their own writing limitations and at times the material makes the rhythm section sound pedestrian. *Tusk* is the sound of a band going one step too far.

A de-luxe version of the album (Warner Bros 8122-73883-2) was released in 2004 and contains the following extra tracks on a second CD of demos, roughs and out-takes: 'One More Time (Over and Over)', 'Can't Walk Out Of Here (The Ledge)', 'Think About Me', 'Sara', 'Lindsey's Song #1 (I Know I'm Not Wrong)', 'Storms', 'Lindsey's Song #2 (That's All For Everyone)', 'Sisters Of The Moon', 'Out On The Road (That's Enough For Me)', 'Brown Eyes', 'Never Make Me Cry', 'Song #1 (I Know I'm Not Wrong)', 'Honey Hi', 'Beautiful Child', 'Song #3', 'Walk A Thin Line', 'Come On Baby (Never Forget)', 'Song #1 (I Know I'm Not Wrong)' [alternate], 'Kiss And Run', 'Farmer's Daughter', 'Think About Me' [single version], 'Sisters Of The Moon' [single version].

OVER AND OVER
(C. McVie)

WITH MUTED guitars, and a slow beat, this makes a pretty but low-key beginning to the double-album. Christine once more casts herself in the role of the Miss Love-Lorn. The title itself was guaranteed to be resonant even if you didn't know what else was going on. The phrase "What can I do to keep you around" is beautifully expressive. Buckingham supplies some slide fills. The backing vocals are sparse and distant, so there's plenty of space. On the coda the title is repeated with some lovely swooping harmonies in the background. It doesn't have anything like the climactic build-up of the live version. A fine if subdued song. Fleetwood is very reserved on the drums. The live version is stronger and bolder.

THE LEDGE
(Buckingham)

THIS QUIRKY arrangement comes complete with prominent bass guitar, minimal drums, and a low guitar line on an instrument that sounds partially de-tuned so the pitch of the notes is odd. There are quirky vocal breaks with whispering. Had it been arranged like a *Rumours* tune, it would have fitted in that album but the intention was to make it different. The overall rhythm is reminiscent of the title track 'Tusk'.

THINK ABOUT ME
(C. McVie)

THIS PUTS us back in familiar Fleetwood Mac territory, with a pumping rhythm section, electric piano and guitar. Christine's double-tracked vocals are supported by Lindsey who is also supplying guitar lead fills. Christine's lyric pleads for her lover to recognise that she needs to be thought of. At the time she had just started an affair with Dennis Wilson of The Beach Boys, so this may be written to him. It's okay, but not up to the standard of 'Over And Over'.

SAVE ME A PLACE
(Buckingham)

CHIMING acoustics lead this slow ballad, as the singer asks his lover not to be turned away. The rhythm is quite clumping and the chorus has very West Coast harmonies that suggest early Neil Young or The Eagles. There's something about the guitar part which may remind some listeners of The Smiths 'I Won't Share You' – possibly the mandolin or the use of Nashville tuning, where the guitar's strings are tuned up an octave to create a high, light, resonant tone. A very melancholy number with slightly gluey vocals on the chorus.

SARA
(Nicks)

WRITTEN about Sara Recor, an old friend of Stevie's, whom Mick Fleetwood later married. It took Fleetwood three days to get the brush work on the drums just right. Bouquets where bouquets are due, 'Sara' is one of the standout tracks on *Tusk* and a deserved hit single in a slightly edited form. It's one small step for Stevie Nicks and one big step for the sisterly comradeship vibe she was cultivating with the female part of her audience. It starts with piano and acoustic guitars before the rhythm section gets the song going on a four-chord turnaround which lilts through Nicks' lyric clichés about 'drowning in a sea of love'. She invites the 'Sara' of the title to call her when she builds her house. Gradually, the band bring up the vocal harmonies in a wonderfully atmospheric arrangement. Nicks' vocal is restrained and hits a beautiful note on the word 'laces'. At the end she builds up the vocal to an elegant climax. The coda attains a hymn-like quality through the harmony vocals on the last repetitions of Sara's name.

The musical complexity goes some way to justifying her winsomeness. The LP cut is longer by a chorus, which is redundant. The single is much better and punchier. A fine example of the band's ability with arrangements and Nicks' strongest song since 'Dreams'.

WHAT MAKES YOU THINK YOU'RE THE ONE
(Buckingham)

A STRANGE drum pattern and clattery sound kick off this track, which has vague associations with The Beach Boys. There are no harmonies on this one and some strange vocal touches by Buckingham, who is evidently trying to do something different with the overall sound to make it more rhythmic and angular. It ends up having something of a throwaway quality about it. It is piano-driven throughout despite the occasional burst of electric guitar, and ends like a rough take.

STORMS
(Nicks)

NICKS' second offering on *Tusk* is a delicate ballad of longing which she sings in her fragile vibrato, supported by electric piano, distant organ, and an interweaving of guitars. The chorus is thick with harmonies. The title isn't borne out by the music. This is not an openly stormy track but instead reflects an inner turmoil. The pay-off line is that she has always been a storm and not a deep blue sea, perhaps with a nod to her restlessness.

The repetition of the line is very effective. Nothing disturbs the level of the track, it maintains a curious calm and resignation. A poignant ultramarine night of a track.

THAT'S ALL FOR EVERYONE
(Buckingham)

THE HOOK-LINE starts this track on an unusual chord change more likely to be heard on a record like Genesis' *Wind And Wuthering*. It's slow, with a *Pet Sounds* influence in the drum-beat, the piano part and harmonies. This is Buckingham's strongest track so far. The chord changes, with the long sustained vocal notes over them, produce quite a heady sense of exhilaration.

NOT THAT FUNNY
(Buckingham)

A PUNCH-and-Judy of a song which Buckingham can be heard milking for all its worth on the *Live* album. It has a club-footed rhythm and deliberate send-up of a ham-fisted boogie, with the guitars having the same odd intonation as on the first track. The overall playing seems amateur, compared to the best of the other songs. But certainly Buckingham gets plenty of mileage out of the hook line. Toward the end the mix becomes quite confusing with a number of different instruments all competing at once. Definitely expendable.

SISTERS OF THE MOON
(Nicks)

THE LYRICS to this were written during the touring of 1975. Another of mystic Stevie's atmospheric hymns to the New Age sisters, this comes in with a slow increase in volume. Buckingham's volume pedal touches recall his playing on 'Dreams'. Nicks uses the black widow image again and describes the entrance of a woman dressed in trailing black who is her dark twin *alter-ego*. It has a slightly turgid quality but would have gone down well in her sisterly circle. Even Buckingham's lyrical guitar touches can't really lift the song, though its live potential is apparent.

ANGEL
(Nicks)

SUSTAINING the stellar imagery of the previous song, Nicks attempts a more uptempo rocking feel for this uninspired track, in which the verse is based on a three-chord trick. Unfortunately, the lyrics come across as merely pretentious and her fey stance looks superficial. The melody sounds somewhat tentative, an impression which the vocal harmonies can't really do anything to remove. For most of the song the backing is thin, and even Buckingham seems at a loss to know what to do. Overall it's a track that never really came together.

THAT'S ENOUGH FOR ME
(Buckingham)

FLEETWOOD slaps the drums four-to-the-bar while Buckingham's guitars and synth work get busy on this fast rocker, which sounds like a country hoedown being played by an electric band. Buckingham has arranged the vocal hook to stretch across an uneven number of bars. The song ends almost as soon as it begins, another throwaway track that doesn't attain its goal.

BROWN EYES
(C. McVie)

THIS VERY subdued ballad has quiet electric piano for the intro and Fleetwood tapping out the beats on a wood-block. A variety of vocal harmonies intertwine on the "sha-la-la" hook. The whole feel is quiet and reserved with a sense of abandonment. Buckingham adds some nice tremolo guitar notes to create a shimmery effect, but the overall performance never really comes together. The chord sequence for the hook is the same as it is for 'Rhiannon'. Fleetwood's occasional ventures into a bar or two of standard drumming always ebb back to the side-drum taps. Another under-achieved song.

NEVER MAKE ME CRY
(C. McVie)

THE SUBDUED mood of the third side of the vinyl album is sustained throughout this ambient ballad. Guitars gently strum the chords and weave a distant counter-melody while Christine McVie patiently takes up her stoic stance of love and promises that he'll never make her cry. It's short, and better than the previous tracks.

I KNOW I'M NOT WRONG
(Buckingham)

SIDE THREE concludes with a bolder uptempo number very much in the style of the upbeat numbers Buckingham contributed to *Rumours*, with electric and acoustic guitars combining. The break is taken by a synth. There's a certain monotony to this song, which stems partly from the rhythm section, especially from the drums, which are pretty much undecorated. Buckingham has two electric guitars soloing through the coda but this still doesn't lift it. Again, a short song.

HONEY HI
(C. McVie)

SIDE FOUR of the vinyl version opens with another Christine McVie song, and from the very first vocal phrases you can tell that inspiration is not going to strike here: the melody is unexciting and the lyrics are full of clichéd images like "sweeter than wine". The verse has a soft shuffle with electric piano, guitars and congas. The band try to build some harmonies from three different groupings before the song fades, like a half-finished track.

BEAUTIFUL CHILD
(Nicks)

A HIGH tinkling piano part over a picked guitar accompanies Nicks singing the title phrase three times and an outbreak of listener wrist-slashing can't be far off. The rhythm is pedestrian, the chord movement uninspired, and Nicks sinks into the abyss of her own maudlin feelings as she wishes this child was hers. Buckingham uses the tremolo guitar effect once more. "I'm not a child any more," sings Nicks, undoing the meaning of her words even as she elaborates. The band plod round the rising three-chord sequence, and things brighten just a little as the intensity picks up and the vocal parts start to multiply. It's another Nicks slow burner. You end up feeling there's a better song in here trying to get out. It fades out instead of coming to any conclusion.

WALK A THIN LINE
(Buckingham)

THIS IS one of those tracks where Fleetwood ends up with his drums sounding like empty suitcases, which is a bit unfortunate. The attractive vocal harmony touches get weighed down by the tempo and the clumping rhythm. After the tonal monotony of some of the other songs, it comes as a bit of a relief to have a key change for the middle passage. The backing vocals have a vaguely tribal quality which lead aptly into 'Tusk'. The main feature here is not Buckingham's guitars, it's the long sustained vocal touches.

TUSK
(Buckingham)

THE ORIGIN of 'Tusk' was in a minute or so of music the band used to jam when the lights went down at the start of their live shows before they hit the first number. Dashut made up a tape loop of a twenty-second version of the four-bar riff. 'Tusk' was a brave choice for a single, given its unorthodoxy, and managed to be a hit. It begins with a tape loop and a quasi-African drum rhythm, over which there's an octave separated vocal melody, supported by acoustic guitar. While the tape loop is still audible, bass and extra drums come in, followed by various cod Indian voices and the University of Southern California's

Trojan 112-piece marching band (recorded live in Dodger Stadium). The hook is interrupted at one point for a drum break, before the band re-enter with a cacophony of brass, whoops and various other instruments, guitars and so on. It's the one moment on the album where Buckingham's production ambitions actually pay off, and a startling sound is achieved. The title, incidentally, has a phallic connotation.

NEVER FORGET
(C. McVie)

A CLASSIC electric piano-driven chord sequence with side-drum ends the album on a higher note. Christine McVie is able to stretch out a little more on this. The refrain of "We'll never forget tonight" is a good party hook, though again the lyrics seem a bit thin. Buckingham adds a slide solo to the acoustic guitar, and there's a hint of swirling keyboard in the background. A gentle slice of rock-'n'roll on which to end this sprawling selection of songs.

Mirage

US Warner Bros 23607 June 1982; UK Warner Bros K 6952;
US CD Warner Bros 23607 2 (1983); UK Warner Bros 256952 (1983);
reissue UK CD Warner Bros K 256592 (1989)

AFTER THE RELEASE OF *TUSK*, FLEETWOOD MAC HAD SIX WEEKS OF REHEARSAL and embarked on a world tour that was eventually captured on a live double album. Hiring an airliner and staying in only the best hotels (redecorating them where necessary) made it ruinously expensive. Afterwards, there were rumours that the band were splitting and various solo projects got under way. Work on *Mirage* was apparently postponed while Stevie Nicks finished her second solo album. The musical ambition expressed on *Tusk* had been abandoned but the material assembled was not especially strong, even to make a standard single record. *Mirage* was an attempt to make a record in the mould of *Rumours*, only updated. Tired of being seen as a Californian hippy, Buckingham wanted to draw on Fifties rock'n'roll. The album illustrates the musical vice of the post-Green Fleetwood Mac, which is that when the songs aren't first class, the band can lack punch and be too polite.

Mirage received a lukewarm reaction from both critics and the band's fans. This didn't stop it making the number 1 slot in the US and number 5 in Britain, and selling about five million copies. The album was recorded at Le Château d'Herouville, France, which is why the penguin mascot on the sleeve is dressed up in a red beret and a striped shirt! The cover showed Stevie Nicks swooning in the arms of Buckingham who is looking over his shoulder at Christine McVie: image-wise, Fleetwood Mac's old game of emotional roulette continued to keep people guessing.

LOVE IN STORE
(C. McVie/Jim Recor)

THE OPENING track is an uptempo, happy, love-song. The lyrics are uninspired, and there's something about Christine's vocals which make them sound less upbeat than the track. The chorus has a certain impact, with a quick succession of chords backed up by patented harmony vocals. Fleetwood drives the track with four-to-the-bar snare. It fades out on some high acoustic guitars and a reverbed solo guitar line.

CAN'T GO BACK
(Buckingham)

BUCKINGHAM'S first contribution to the record has a synthesised feel, due to the quaver synth percussion recorded with a stereo delay. Otherwise, there's acoustic guitar, and Buckingham handles most of the backing vocals. The lyrics describe a conflict of emotion – the singer wants to return to an old flame but realises that it isn't possible. The imagery refers to a dream maker, so listeners could be forgiven for thinking it referred to Stevie Nicks.

THAT'S ALRIGHT
(Nicks)

TALKING of whom... Nicks' opening contribution is a country-sounding song with her voice crystal-clear in the mix. When the chorus comes in, there's a thick wash of harmonies and a pedal-steel guitar in the background. A distant organ complemented by honky-tonk piano and several acoustic guitars. The melody never really achieves much of a memorable shape. The best moment is when Nicks breaks away from the tune to hit some higher notes. A West Coast Eagles-type song.

BOOK OF LOVE
(Buckingham/R. Dashut)

THE TITLE refers back to an old Fifties tune, 'Book Of Love' by The Monotones (1958), mentioned in the lyric and developed with the imagery of the torn page. Musically, a simple song with a four-to-the bar

snare from Fleetwood, full harmonies, and a delivery from Buckingham which, despite being passionate, doesn't manage to lift the song from being ordinary. He gets in a brief solo at the coda, but take-off is never quite achieved.

GYPSY
(Nicks)

THIS IS AN uptempo country-ish number with some chiming picked arpeggios, and rising and falling harmonies in the background. The melody begins low, then slowly gets pitched higher and higher. The lyric seems to be addressed to a character she perceives as part of herself. This figure was there in the past, is now going, and was loved by someone now lost. The imagery is typically romantic with lightning, dancing, children, and bright eyes. The pay-off line is: "it all comes down to you". There's a sensitive solo from Buckingham just before the fade. Another track that seems to wilt rather than conclude.

ONLY OVER YOU
(C. McVie)

THIS IS strongly reminiscent of several of McVie's *Tusk* tracks because of its two-chord sequence for the first part of the verse. The overall feel is typical Mac, but there's also a slight Beach Boys influence, which is appropriate owing to the song's dedication "with special thanks for inspiration to Dennis Wilson", with whom Christine McVie was having a relationship. This is easily the strongest track on side one of the album. There's a pleasant solo to end it on the fade.

EMPIRE STATE
(Buckingham)

HAD LINDSEY relocated? This song is lyrically based on a contrast between Fleetwood Mac's stomping ground LA and New York, here represented by that monolithic tribute to art deco, the Empire State Building. Buckingham asks the city to let him be what he wants to be. The vocal is double-tracked and distant, and the arrangement is stripped down and sparse, with very subdued guitar. A little phasing on the vocals is used to illustrate the "flying high" line. The robotic drumming makes the whole a bit stiff and lifeless. Not a very strong opener for the second side. The only point of interest is the curious tone of the stringed instrument being struck on the outro.

STRAIGHT BACK
(Nicks)

THIS HAS a minor key descending sequence and Nicks singing low.
Nicks breaks Rule 5 in the book of *How To Write A Great Song*: never write lyrics about writing a song as this almost always means the song will turn out fit only to be served on a plate at Thanksgiving. (The only honourable exception that springs to mind is Elton John's 'Your Song'.) Scientists are still trying to find out why this should be so. 'Straight Back' is more woolly than a Siberian mammoth. It may reduce your heating bills in the winter.

HOLD ME
(C. McVie/Robbie Patton)

THE FIRST of the two hit singles from the album. Over a medium tempo rock'n'roll pattern Buckingham and McVie share the vocals on this tale of love gone wrong. The chorus climbs up its chord sequence with some interesting pizzicato arpeggios, some on guitar. Buckingham contributes another high-pitched melodic solo before there's a pause for the piano. It's an average Fleetwood Mac performance and never really catches fire.

OH DIANE
(Buckingham)

THE OLD doo-wop chord-sequence of I-VI-IV-V is resurrected for this somewhat anaemic nod back to early Sixties teen ballads, in particular Neil Sedaka and Bobby Vee. The backing is minimal and very controlled. It's commercial but a cream-puff. Buckingham apes the slightly falsetto vocal characteristics of the early Sixties singers.

EYES OF THE WORLD
(Buckingham)

THERE'S A quiet intro to this number but it soon goes up a gear when Buckingham comes in with a more committed vocal and the drums start hammering away in pronounced stereo. This comes across as having benefited a little from *Tusk*. There's a pleasing guitar break where an electric lead is combined with some harmonised acoustic lead. The backing vocals are so far back in the mix as to be almost inaudible. Some of the guitar work suggests the influence of Andy Summer's muted arpeggios with The Police. The song comes to a forceful ending with Buckingham's solo. It's not a great song but at least it has more energy, and a sudden ending to boot.

WISH YOU WERE HERE
(C. McVie/Colin Allen)

THE ALBUM ends with another melancholic ballad from Christine McVie. Colin Allen's lyrics are no more inspired than her own. The verse has some pretty descending changes, and the chorus is decorated by some hymnal backing vocals as the melody goes to its predictable conclusion. The middle eight moves to the minor and then heads back again. The rhythm section stay on the beat and rarely deviate from holding down the pulse, with the consequence of making things sound a bit flat-footed. One of the stronger tracks on an album not especially blessed with good songs.

Tango In The Night

US Warner Bros 1-25471; UK Warner Bros WX 65 April 1987;
US CD Warner Bros 254712;UK CD Warner Bros 9254712 (1987)

IN THE LATE SEVENTIES AND EARLY EIGHTIES FLEETWOOD MAC ENJOYED EVERY luxury a band could dream of on tour. Mick Fleetwood has described how they would get off the plane and walk to 14 limousines. Needless to say, public acclaim, and lots of folding stuff, hardly did much for the size of their egos, and inter-band harmony suffered. In the early Eighties, first Nicks and then Buckingham were embroiled in solo careers, the former attracting speculation that she was becoming a rock'n'roll casualty.

Tango in the Night took five years to put together. The story goes that the band was drawn together again almost by accident. Nicks was recording Presley's 'Can't Help Falling In Love' for a film, and she asked Buckingham to play guitar on it. He in turn brought in McVie and Fleetwood to play on the session. Thus most of the group found themselves working together again.

Buckingham interrupted his third solo album in order to oversee the creation of *Tango*, agreeing to be involved with the proviso that he would leave as soon as it was done. Fleetwood tells a different story of a stormy meeting on August 7 1987, with Buckingham pulling out after tour dates were established. Nicks, we are told, took it especially badly and a fight ensued which attained an almost homicidal intensity.

The album shows the Mac formula tarted up for the end of the Eighties but with even less emotional resonance than on earlier albums. After the sprawling ambition of *Tusk* and the double live album, the band wisely decided to continue *Mirage*'s attempt to trim things back. Everything here is lightweight, undemanding and unrewarding. That didn't prevent its commercial success. The album made number 1 on both sides of the Atlantic, and returned to the number 1 slot during the band's UK tour supporting it. No less than five tracks from it made the UK chart, including three in the Top 10: 'Big Love', 'Everywhere' and 'Little Lies'. The cover featured a painting, 'Homage to Henri Rousseau' by Brett-Livingstone Strong, and was dedicated to Judy Wong.

BIG LOVE
(Buckingham)

A BRISK stereo beat shows the effect of drum-programming on this song. The verse is short and puts Buckingham's voice to the front. There are some nice touches of rubbery acoustic guitar, and some stylised grunts and groans generated by messing about with the composer's voice. Buckingham supports the song with a solo played at the edge of feedback. The coda takes over for a prominent bit of drumming. Certainly a more confident opening track than a Fleetwood Mac had delivered for a while. The video for this track cost a cool quarter of a million dollars.

SEVEN WONDERS
(Sandy Stewart/ additional words Nicks)

A SYNTH line at the start keeps the contemporary feel, and the drum beat is punchier than in many Mac productions. Nicks sings with more energy, but doesn't have much of a tune, and her singing is still somewhat mannered. The lyrics offer plenty of naff pseudo-mystical imagery. She can also be heard singing 'Sara' in between the choruses and verses. 'Fey' doesn't come more professional than this.

EVERYWHERE
(C. McVie)

A GLITTERY beginning with various synth keyboards before the muted guitars and the typical Eighties hard snare drum tone come in. Neither the lyrics nor the melody are of any great interest. There's a feeling of Christine McVie's song being airbrushed by the production. The glittery beginning is reprised for the middle break before the last verse. The coda has some abrupt voices calling and answering across the stereo field, which may well have been sampled.

CAROLINE
(Buckingham)

A N UNDISTINGUISHED effort, this is initially driven by a rhythmic quasi-African drum sound which comes back for the chorus, where Buckingham sings the name Caroline (a Brian Wilson allusion) with his voice tracked several times. The guitars are very spare on this. The lyric seems to be driven by its own rhymes. This is probably the strongest track so far, though the arrangement somehow short-changes the power of it. Listen out for the female voice that wordlessly intones over the drums at the end as Buckingham sings "what have I done".

TANGO IN THE NIGHT
(Buckingham)

THE INTRO of this number has a sparkling arrangement. The song has a radical shift of atmosphere between the verse, which is romantic and reflective, and the descending chord sequence; and the chorus, which is punchier, and climaxes with Buckingham holding a note for about four long bars. It's not what you'd expect for the title track. There's a heavy guitar section with the rhythm section making its presence felt more. 'Tango In The Night' is a song that would obviously work well live. More attention should have been given to the backing over which the solo is played.

MYSTIFIED
(Buckingham/C. McVie)

THE LYRIC on this number is tissue thin, but they manage to concoct a pretty ballad out of it with McVie taking the lead vocal and Buckingham adding backing vocals. The guitar solo floats away in the reverb. It has an ethereal, dreamy atmosphere. If only Peter Green had been on hand to do something with this.

LITTLE LIES
(C. McVie/Eddy Quintela)

A SYNTH intro that recalls mid-Seventies Genesis quickly passes into a very confident verse with a few synth pads. The chorus has plenty of high range effects, and Buckingham and Nicks' voices stand out as the others add the harmonies. The synth intro comes back again in the middle, complete with wind-chimes adding top-range glitter. The verse has some clever vocal ideas. The chorus is very catchy, and really stands out in the way it emphasises the band's identity. 'Little Lies' is more upbeat than McVie's material often is. The album's stand-out track and the band's biggest single in the UK since the days of Green, reaching number five.

FAMILY MAN
(Buckingham/R. Dashut)

THE SYNTH chords on the chorus of this number are reminiscent of The Human League, of all people, and the lyrics are rather clichéd. There's even a Spanish guitar solo after the first chorus. A good example of professional music-making which never gets further. Any real individual expression has got lost. The Spanish solo is reprised twice more over the quick, tight rhythm of the backing. The speaker seems trapped in the circle of the lyrics and unable to articulate it any further.

WELCOME TO THE ROOM... SARA
(Nicks)

APPARENTLY, when Nicks checked into the Betty Ford Center she used the name of Sara Anderson. There is a harshness to her vocal on this track which is not pleasing. Despite the effort of the production the song is undistinguished. You even get a quote from Cat Stevens' 'The First Cut Is The Deepest'. The verse simply doesn't have a melody. Not a very effective number.

ISN'T IT MIDNIGHT
(C. McVie/Quintela/Buckingham)

THIS HAS a beefy MOR production with twin electric rhythm guitars and a strong drum rhythm. The guitar solo is what you would expect. The synth arpeggio on the verse is the AOR staple, with the piano supplying high frequency notes. This is the strongest song on the second side. It's more muscular than you expect Christine McVie's stuff to be, and features the sort of coda solo that could be elongated live in concert *ad infinitum*. The solo dissolves in incoherence with a dodgy sequence of consecutive fourths.

WHEN I SEE YOU AGAIN
(Nicks)

THIS IS A quiet ballad opening with acoustic guitars and strings, with Nicks' voice right to the fore. Nicks manages to reduce the lyric to gibberish repeating 'baby' in half a dozen different tones, all of them equally brain-damaged. This treatment of the chorus is so awful it kills the song dead in its tracks. The middle eight gives you a Springsteenish melody. The only lift comes when Buckingham makes a contribution to the song, adding the twist about them once having been lovers. Nicks doesn't answer Buckingham, but remains silent. There's an acoustic guitar solo and then it fades away. It's kind of a successor to 'Landslide'.

YOU AND I, PART II
(Buckingham/McVie)

THE TITLE is an 'in' joke, since Part 1 was the B-side of the 'Little Lies' single. Buckingham takes the lead vocal over a medium tempo verse until the chorus. There's a bizarre hook which involves the word 'you' being split across the stereo mix, giving a decidedly synthetic feel. There is a strong hint of early Beach Boys in the melody at the end of the verse. A lightweight song that ends the album on a listenable note.

Behind The Mask

US Warner Bros 1-266111 April 1990; UK Warner Bros WX 335 April 1990;
US CD Warner Bros 9-26111-2 (1990); UK CD Warner Bros 7599261112;
US CD; limited ed box set Warner Bros 9-26206-2 (1990)
UK 759926206-2

FLEETWOOD MAC ENTERED THE NINETIES WITH SOME IMPORTANT PERSONNEL changes. After Lindsey Buckingham's departure, the band recruited two guitarists, Rick Vito and Billy Burnette, to fill his place, and set off on a ten-week *Shake The Cage* tour of the US. Burnette came from a band called The Zoo, while Vito was an LA guitar expert. On tour the rhythm section was augmented by Ghanaian percussionist Isaac Asante who met Mick Fleetwood on one of the latter's trips to West Africa. This line-up then went into the studios and made this album.

The production on *Behind The Mask* is lush, but the songs are nothing to write home about. Neither Christine McVie nor Stevie Nicks could offer material to match the best of their earlier work, and the new boys do not bring in any gems. Instead, there's a bit more mainstream rock widdling; a move away from the pop sensibility of *Rumours*, and from a West Coast sound, to Bryan Adams-type corporate rock. Fleetwood Mac had, of course, been purveyors of corporate rock for quite some time, but they had always done it with a certain breezy charm. *Behind The Mask* is fairly charmless. The band's musical identity has been diluted.

Fleetwood Mac toured extensively, played 10 nights at the Wembley Arena in London, and released a *Greatest Hits* (1988) before releasing *Behind The Mask* in 1990. The album went to number 1 in the UK, and, in 1990, the band sold out Wembley Stadium, which proved that they could still command a wide audience. Around this time Christine McVie and Stevie Nicks announced that they would be leaving the band as far as live shows were concerned, though they would continue to record with them.

SKIES THE LIMIT
(C. McVie/E.Quintela)

THE ALBUM kicks off with some ethnic-sounding synth settings making an intricate intro before the first song kicks in. It's an upbeat, optimistic rock number, with some long sustained guitar notes decorating it. Nicks shares the lead vocal with Christine McVie. The middle eight goes into half time. The drum sound is noticeably bigger, and the overall sound more produced. There's a smooth, short guitar solo using the E-bow, a device which is held in the hand close to the strings of the guitar and causes the string to vibrate and thus produce a sustained note. The outro is longer than the old Fleetwood Mac would have allowed.

LOVE IS DANGEROUS
(Rick Vito/S. Nicks)

SOME BLUESY guitar licks open this rock number with Nicks and Vito sharing the vocals. There are bursts of slide guitar over the sub-Stevie Ray Vaughan riffs. This has a tougher sound than many Fleetwood Mac tracks, so much so that Nicks sounds a little adrift in the mix. The guitar break in the middle is panned left right and centre in the mix during a single run, which is a neat trick. The chorus is not much of a hook and neither are the blues intervals throughout the melody. It comes to an unexpected halt.

IN THE BACK OF MY MIND
(Billy Burnette/David Malloy)

ANOTHER slightly 'ethnic' sounding intro, with a repeated tom-tom pattern, wind-chimes, and a triangle creating the backdrop for some slowed-down voices. A gong sounds and the strings rise. It's a dense, atmospheric arrangement, recalling the Mac of *Tusk*. After a while, much of this backing fades into a normal rock arrangement with a flowing guitar solo, which leads into the first verse whose melody and vocal melody sound

like a slowed-down Bryan Adams ('Everybody Needs Somebody'). Nicks counterpoints the tune with a harmony. The feel is not dissimilar to that of 'Rhiannon', but this is not as strong a song. Christine McVie takes on the middle eight, which has a dramatic effect of contrast. The song then returns briefly to the atmospheric intro. Very much an attempt at an epic, it never manages to be more than the sum of its parts. The inclusion of plenty of guitar soloing at the end increases the impression that the band are losing their pop sensibility.

DO YOU KNOW
(Billy Burnette/Christine McVie)

A BEVY OF acoustic guitars and not a lot else usher in the shared vocal by the songwriters. A slow, mellow song with little sparse touches in the arrangement, and a touch of colour here and there. Soft drums support the chorus. The lyric is deeply uninteresting – not even a hint of a metaphor anywhere. Congas add a nice touch on the percussion front, and there's an acceptable guitar break in the middle, but it's no great shakes as a song.

SAVE ME
(McVie/Quintela)

A PRETTY atmospheric beginning leads into a sparser driving beat, which is curiously reminiscent of an early Madonna single until Christine McVie starts singing. The verse is carried by electric guitar power chords, electric piano and distant strings. The chorus is quite commercial, but sounds like Madonna's 'Holiday' speeded up. This is an attempt to capture the light-rocking Fleetwood Mac, but the production and the banked vocals are standard MOR. There's a horrible widdly guitar solo that could be anyone, and damped single lines underneath it. This is muddy and turgid 'rawck'.

AFFAIRS OF THE HEART
(Nicks)

F ULL-ON jangly guitars start this Nicks composition, which is sung in her inimitable style (ahem). Contrary to what the title might lead you to expect, this is an upbeat, almost country-rock song with Nicks harmonising with her own and others' voices. The melody of the verse is juxtaposed with a 12-string guitar riff, leaving gaps between the vocals, which has the unfortunate effect of lengthening the verse. The guitar section matches a Duane Eddy tremolo break with several higher guitars, which produces a muddy sound. The hook line

of the song – "It's better to have loved and lost than never to have loved at all" – was in fact penned by Victorian poet/superstar Sir Alfred Lord Tennyson, and is taken from a track on his concept album *In Memoriam* (1850).

WHEN THE SUN GOES DOWN
(Vito/Burnette)

A SLICE of country 'rawck' complete with the shuffly drums, harmonica, acoustic guitars and harmonised vocals. The lyric clichés are all present and correct, SIR! You know how you sometimes find yourself watching a film with no-one famous in it which you don't really want to watch, and two of the characters go off to meet at a barn-dance party? Well, the music that the band at the barn-dance party will be playing will sound exactly like this. Those who wish to predict the future of Fleetwood Mac on the basis of the input of the new boys need look no further.

BEHIND THE MASK
(C. McVie)

T HIS TRACK features Lindsey Buckingham playing some delicate finger-picked guitar. A hi-tech wash of strings and various other sustained chords create an unusual backing for Christine's voice. Lyrically, the song deals with the problem of assessing the offers of an old lover who wants to return – an angel in black who is the devil in disguise. Buckingham takes an acoustic guitar solo which is effective enough. The general impression is of a lot going on in the arrangement. It sounds like two tracks were given up to the Coral sitar guitar. Just on the fade you can hear one of Buckingham's trademark single-note phrases. Although imaginative, it's not really strong enough to be the title track.

STAND ON THE ROCK
(Rick Vito)

Vito's GUITAR arpeggio and low string riffs are very much out of the Bryan Adams' songbook, (i.e. half way to AC/DC) and the lyrics are pretty much the same – clichés delivered with a breathless disregard for any known Muse or source of inspiration. This is very average, and the production can't conceal it. It's even got the bit where the vocal hook alternates with a couple of drum fills. Your love is like the sea... Quite. We're going by hovercraft.

HARD FEELINGS
(Billy Burnette/Jeff Silbar)

An echoed synth melody line breaks into a wash of sound and a verse which uses a descending chromatic sequence – perhaps just a tad influenced by Led Zep's 'Kashmir'. The chorus sounds a little like Phil Collins and late Genesis.

Lyrically, a song about two lovers who have split up, leaving him with... hard feelings. The chromatic verse contrasts with the major/minor chord sequence of the chorus which is quite long. There's a harmonised guitar solo over the verse sequence before some synth brass leads into the last chorus. Certainly better than Vito's offering.

FREEDOM
(Nicks/Mike Campbell)

Here Nicks co-writes with Tom Petty's main side-kick. The song comes thumping in at quite a lick after 'Hard Feelings', with a minor key verse decorated with a few guitar licks. The chord sequence on the chorus is an AOR staple, the same as was used in 'Rhiannon'. Nicks turns in a vocal which isn't too encrusted with her mannerisms. The rhythm pauses for the middle eight, which then leads into a solo full of country-style bending. Asante plays percussion on this track. The rhythm section sound a lot happier here, and I should think it would go down well in concert. Shades of the live 'Rhiannon' are quite strong on the fade-out.

WHEN IT COMES TO LOVE
(Burnette/Dennis Morgan/
Simon Climie)

A DELICATE intro leads to a verse where Burnette and McVie share the vocals. This is another track that tries to recapture the classic Fleetwood Mac sound, complete with block harmonies on the chorus. The middle eight has some dense overlays of melody before the acoustic guitar solo. Not particularly inspired as a song though one of the more listenable on the album.

THE SECOND TIME
(Nicks/Vito)

SIX-STRING and 12-string acoustics start this song by putting a chiming curtain behind Nicks' slurred singing. This is a slow ballad about the possibility of rekindling a relationship. A synth melody counterpoints the main tune which isn't much of a tune. This is the shortest track on the record.

Time

Warner CD 9362-45920-2; released 1995

FLEETWOOD MAC'S SECOND ALBUM OF THE NINETIES SAW ANOTHER LINE-UP change. Stevie Nicks left and was replaced by the younger and more earthy Bekka Bramlett on vocals. The album shows the band moving further away from their classic Seventies sound, but the rhythm section of Fleetwood/McVie alone doesn't have quite enough identity to make the band unmistakable. New boys Burnette and Sixties veteran Dave Mason (who replaced De Vito) pull the band more toward a standardised rock. Only the tracks with Christine McVie on vocals sound like the old Fleetwood Mac.

Time was undistinguished in its material, and, like many albums of the CD era, at least 15 minutes too long. The times given to the songs on the sleeve make this point eloquently. The Christine McVie/Eddy Quintela partnership produced five tracks, while the remaining eight came from a whole range of writers. This goes some way to explaining the lack of focus and the mainstream blandness of so much of the material, especially in the lyric department.

TALKIN' TO MY HEART
*(Burnette/Deborah Allen/
Rafe VanHoy)*

A BURST OF furiously strummed guitars on a descending sequence gives way to a verse in which Burnette and Bramlett share vocals with some nice 'violin'-guitar note touches. After the chorus, the volume drops again to finger-picked guitar, the violin effect and Fleetwood's distant rattling hi-hat. Unfortunately, this could be any American band. There's a slight country flavour to this track which could, unfortunately, be by any American band. Only Christine McVie's occasional backing vocals give it any real character. An average start.

HOLLYWOOD
(C. McVie/Eddy Quintela)

T HE GUITARS on this track are provided by Michael Thompson. This is another medium-uptempo pop number, on which the guitars are joined by an electric piano. Christine McVie takes the vocal, singing a song of alienation from the city and a distant lover. The chorus has a block harmony providing an antiphonal response to the lead vocal. Christine's voice retains its English feel as she extols the virtue of living somewhere where the seasons are more defined than in Southern California. Christine, what can we say? Huddersfield, Bletchley and Warminster await your return with open arms. The arrangement is tight – notice the way John McVie's bass hugs the second and fourth beats through much of it – but it never really inspires. Another average number.

BLOW BY BLOW
(Dave Mason/John Cesario/ Mark Holden)

READ THE lyric sheet and count the clichés: "backs against the wall", "make a stand", and the title itself. The song is possibly about lovers fighting the world or each other and not giving up. Especially not giving up. Check out Elvis Costello's 'Beaten To The Punch' for what can be done with that phrase. 'Blow By Blow' is a medium-paced rocker with a slightly noisier drum sound and more distorted guitars. After a gospel-like second chorus, we get a nice middle-eight with some pleasing minor chords. The whole is decorated with predictable lead lines. A stodgy lurch toward Bryan Adams – and perhaps the track that sounds least like Fleetwood Mac.

WINDS OF CHANGE
(Kit Hain)

CAN YOU believe it? Only the five millionth pop song to use the phrase 'winds of change'. Don't these people know the meaning of the word cliché?

Bekka steps up to the mike to sing this lamentable cheer-up song. The relationship is over, but change is going to make things better. Acoustic guitars right and left give the minor-chord laden sequence a chiming quality. We get an average guitar solo before the last verse. She has a tendency to sound like a backing vocalist on stand-by for Foreigner for whenever they decide to follow up 'I Want To Know What Love Is'. This track keeps to its dynamic level and then fades.

I DO
(C. McVie/Eddy Quintela)

PIANO kicks off this track, which quickly settles down into a two-chord change with some muted guitar. It's pleasant to hear Christine McVie, so often Miss Love Lorn, purveyor of sad tunes, write a happy love-song. The chorus slips into a nice half-time feel for the first two phrases, and there are a number of minor chords put in just to up the emotional ante, with full backing vocals. The verse comes close to emulating the mid-Seventies Fleetwood Mac sound. The chorus chord sequence owes a little to the more baroque Motown hits of the Sixties. There's a nasty guitar break using a strange pitch-shifting device, possibly one of those horrible tube things with which Peter Frampton used to clean his teeth in the Seventies.

NOTHING WITHOUT YOU
(Delaney Bramlett/
Doug Gilmore/Bekka Bramlett)

A SLIDE guitar riff leads into an uptempo piano and acoustic driven song of lurve and dedication sung by Bekka Bramlett. More gospel-sounding vocal harmonies come in here and there, which give the band quite a different sound and are strange when juxtaposed with the harmonies provided by Christine McVie on the opposite side of the mix. There are touches here of Maria McKee and the countryside of Lone Justice. Bekka Bramlett emotes in a far more soul oriented feel than either Stevie or Christine.

DREAMIN' THE DREAM
(Bekka Bramlett/Billy Burnette)

A T LAST, a lull in the bouncy popcorn. Over two acoustic guitars and mandolin, Bekka sings a very countryish ballad in which she nurtures the flame of their relationship and what they had, until he returns. There's an accordion-like sound in the back of the mix. Its chief virtue is its brevity.

SOONER OR LATER
(Christine McVie/Eddy Quintela)

THE THIRD McVie/Quintela composition on the album, 'Sooner Or Later' begins with a low bass note, a descending high guitar figure, before the other instruments start layering things. Here Christine is singing about a lover from the past. We have a selection of the usual lyric touches about summer/winter/day/night/dreams. The chorus climbs up supported by some classic block harmonies in the old Mac tradition. This is one of the stronger tracks on a weak album. It's also one of the longest tracks, and illustrates the need for pruning, since it has a lengthy instrumental coda. One of those endings which have been written with one eye (or ear) on the live stage.

I WONDER WHY
(Dave Mason/Frank Previte/
Tom Fuller)

A N UPTEMPO song with either Mason or Burnette on vocals, in which the verse bounces along on a minor chord with acoustic guitars. The chorus goes to a half-time feel, as the voice laments the end of a relationship, and his determination that it won't put him under. The chorus is built on a descending sequence. Bekka throws in the occasional harmony and answer phrase, especially on the middle eight, and there are a number of lead breaks.

NIGHTS IN ESTORIL
(Christine McVie/Eddy Quintela)

THE FOURTH offering from McVie/Quintela, this opens with lush string and vocal pads and cymbals, and then gets going in a reasonably paced Mac groove. Christine McVie deploys several of her melodic trademarks. The chorus features the exotic setting of Estoril, a beach resort near Lisbon in Portugal, which almost offsets the clichés elsewhere, like "how could something so right/Be so wrong". Answers to this box number...

This is the strongest of their featured compositions, and the one that most powerfully evokes the *Rumours* period because of its images and the backing vocals. There are two guitar solos on this number, which is one too many.

I GOT IT IN FOR YOU
(Billy Burnette/Deborah Allen)

THIS STARTS with a twisted single note blues riff and then settles down to a bluesy shuffle in E with the vocals shared between Burnette and Bramlett which again takes them into Bryan Adams territory. Among many contenders, the stand-out cliché is "runnin' undercover in the darkness of the night". You won't be surprised to know there's a slide guitar break. Mediocre.

ALL OVER AGAIN
(Christine McVie/Eddy Quintela)

FIFTH contribution: a song about lovers saying goodbye but always remembering each other. A

pretty burst of orchestral strings gives way to electric piano and a hammock of a chord sequence going down and then up. It has a reasonable hook. This is slow three-time giving a distinctive lilt which is welcome after the rest of the 4/4 stuff. Mac watchers will enjoy the allusion to breaking the chain. Guitars by Michael Thompson, who adds some nice acoustic touches. One track that isn't over-long.

THESE STRANGE TIMES
(Mick Fleetwood/Ray Kennedy)

THE ALBUM'S most glaring example of over-reaching, as Mick Fleetwood (no less) intones in best mid-Seventies prog-rock manner a song about spiritual desolation and conflict, with several clear allusions to Peter Green, the 'Green Manalishi' and 'Man Of The World'. It starts with African percussion, a cello line and sustained synth string pads. Fleetwood speaks the words in a politely portentous manner. "God is nowhere" ends the first verse. A voice calls out "Daddy, hold on, God is now here". The music is inadequate to capture the emotion of spiritual conflict and at seven minutes, the track is far too long. The third verse is supported by drums and kicks along. The imagery is simplistic. The track only serves to remind us how great Green's best songs were in the way they presented an unpolished expression of these emotions. At least this track's heart is in the right place.

Say You Will

Reprise CD 9362-484792; DVD-A; released 2003

PRODUCED MOSTLY BY LINDSEY BUCKINGHAM WITH ASSISTANCE FROM ROB Cavallo and John Shanks. Recorded at The Bellagio House, Ocean Way Recording, Lindsey's garage and Cornerstone Recording Studios. Additional performers were Sheryl Crow, Christine McVie, Jamie Muhoberac, Dave Palmer, John Pierce and John Shanks.

Fleetwood Mac's first album of a new century saw four-fifths of the *Rumours* line-up reunited. Christine McVie decided she didn't want to re-join the band although she is credited among the musicians. Her earthy elegance is noticeable by its absence, especially over this length of record. Buckingham told the *New York Daily News* (April 2003) that without her "the remaining musicians had 33 1/3rd % more room to maneouvre. We were able to flex our muscles and explore a more masculine sound. It's closer to what we're like live." Nicks told *Performing Songwriter* Magazine (May 2003), "Taking away the piano made the whole music tend to focus more on a guitar-oriented thing, which is great."

The roots of this album lie in Buckingam's plans for a solo album and calling up Mick and John to play on it. They enjoyed it so much it made them re-consider the band's position. Mick Fleetwood told *Uncut* magazine (May 2003), "I thought I was going to spend three weeks doing overdubs on Lindsey's album. My whole thing is Fleetwood Mac forever. But I prefaced my renewed relationship with Lindsey by saying, 'You know I want Fleetwood Mac back together. But I don't want you thinking that's why I'm here.' But it went so well that it was Lindsey who said maybe we could turn this into a Fleetwood Mac record." Nicks was about to go on tour for her solo album *Trouble In Shangri-La*. She gave the band a CD of 17 songs so they could listen and select a few for the record.

Not all the material is up to the standard of their best mid-Seventies music, and at 76 minutes it is almost a double album, when a single album of about 40 minutes might have been more potent. In fact at one stage it was going to be a full-blown double but five songs were cut to fit it on a single disc. But it's an album that will please fans because there's enough trademarks present. *Say You Will* is a much better record than many would have expected at this point in their career. As usual Fleetwood and McVie do their job so well that you hardly stop to listen to them. Buckingham's guitar-playing retains its character, as do Nicks' melodies and lyrics.

The expanded edition has four additonal tracks: 'Not Make Believe', 'Love Minus Zero/No Limit' by Bob Dylan, and live versions of 'Peacekeeper' and 'Say You Will'.

WHAT'S THE WORLD COMING TO
(Lindsey Buckingham, Julian Raymond)

LISTEN FOR the roomy drum sound at the very beginning. Upbeat song in F major expressing disillusionment as Lindsey Buckingham muses on a world in which there's only greed and in the personal sphere 'a house filled with shame'. The opening verse is carried by acoustic guitars and organ. The chorus has a low-pitched melody and a nice counter-pointed lead guitar phrase. After chorus two there's a brief guitar solo. Nicks sings multi-tracked backing vocals generally under the lead vocal, panned hard right on the bridge. The chorus' lyric alludes to Jonathan King's 1965 hit 'Everyone's Gone To The Moon'. Buckingham's long-held notes on the coda sound reminiscent of Michael Stipe of R.E.M.

MURROW TURNING OVER IN HIS GRAVE
(Lindsey Buckingham)

LISTENERS who didn't grow up in America may be puzzled as to the identity of the Murrow who is turning in his grave. The man in question is Ed Murrow (1908-1965) who was a journalist and broadcaster during the Forties and Fifties, working for CBS. In 1961 he was appointed Director of the US Information Agency for the Kennedy administration. A man with liberal political views, he had a formidable reputation for the integrity of his work. Buckingham (May 2003) recalled that it had been inspired, "by watching TV and seeing what it's become, how horrendous it's become as a tool to do exactly what Edward R. Murrow warned against when he gave his famous speech. He said if TV is allowed to distract and delude people, then there will be a large price to pay down the line."

An imaginative track, this opens with a two-bar acoustic guitar finger-picked riff. Buckingham uses a breathless, agitated falsetto for the vocal. There's a great drum intro after each chorus and a feast of weird guitar lead lines over on the left after the choruses. The chorus has multiple vocal melody lines. The drums have a lot more reverb than on track 1, creating a more muscular beat. The guitar solo has the kind of distortion that results from plugging straight into a mixing desk and is played with heavy echo, with the pick creating percussive clicks. Underneath this solo there are speaking voices left and right, one of which might be Murrow.

ILLUME (9-11)
(Stevie Nicks)

LET NICKS explain: "I wrote it because I had arrived in New York at 3 o'clock in the morning, in the middle of the night, and had gone to the Waldorf Astoria hotel and got there at 4.30 and then unpacked, went to bed at 7.30, and then somewhere between 10.30 and 11 my assistant came in and tapped me on the shoulder and said, 'I think you need to wake up and see what's happening'. And so I was in New York for three days, and it was so disturbing, and 'Illume' was a poem that I wrote when I got back to Los Angeles at the end of that tour. There was part of me that thought I might never get home. It was so frightening out there... I'm very, very proud of that song. I wanted to say something for those people [New Yorkers] that would be forever."

'Illume' has an exotic rhythm pattern and the kind of open-tuned acoustic guitar riff that is a speciality of Jimmy Page. Buckingham helps with backing vocals on the left. There's a multi-voiced interlude and high-pitched lead outbursts that are intended to have an Indian character. This is a 9/11 song which despite its somewhat monotonous melody avoids sentimentality and compares well with Springsteen's responses on *The Rising*.

THROWN DOWN
(Stevie Nicks)

NICKS HAS said this song was written around 1997, the time of *The Dance*. This takes the album onto more familiar musical territory. It's a standard Nicks love song with some classic changes around F minor. A glassy, echoed guitar figure

carries the verse and lifts the chorus. This has the feel of classic breezy radio-friendly Mac from the mid-Seventies. Buckingham sings backing vocal on verse two. This is perhaps the first track on the album where the third voice of Christine McVie is noticeable in its absence.

MIRANDA
(Lindsey Buckingham)

'MIRANDA' is the second track based on an acoustic guitar riff, with Lindsey and Stevie sharing the vocals. Buckingham plays some nice slide on this, as well as some faster fuzzy lead which interacts with the other parts in the mix rather than being intended to stand on its own. Lyrically, it's a portrait of an unhappy enigmatic female who is alone despite the celebrity status signified by seeing her face in a magazine. Some of the high lead guitar parts have a mildly exotic 'Eastern' feel because of the slide slurs.

RED ROVER
(Lindsey Buckingham)

BUCKINGHAM told Canadian writer Ritchie Yorke that this was his favourite track from *Say You Will*, pointing out that it was "very much a simple guitar part doing the work of the whole rhythm track to a great degree. That's the kind of thing that interests me at the moment." 'Red Rover' opens with frantic, choppy acoustic guitar filtered in a pseudo-tremolo effect. It's not immediately apparent where the beat is. Gradually the fast triple time becomes apparent. The vocals are pulled a long way back in the mix. The chorus has a strange, virtually one-note octave chant with Buckingham at the lower end of his range, contrasting the high voice Buckingham employs on the verse. Musically, it's very much one from the experimental Buckingham songbook. From 3:20 to the end there's a fine, watery texture to the arrangement. It has been suggested that this is a political song, but if so obscurity masks the details.

SAY YOU WILL
(Stevie Nicks)

TITLE-TRACK and one of the album's singles, 'Say You Will' brings the rhythm section back in for the kind of straight-ahead rock song that the Mac specialise in. The lyric might be interpreted as a song about Buckingham, but Nicks has also said in interviews that it was partly directed at Christine. Nicks told Bill DeMain, "when you like somebody it makes you a different person ... It's about a movie I saw about Arthuro Sandoval, the trumpet player."

The electric guitar is pulled back in the mix on the right. The chorus has an optimistic climbing progression that continues going up a little longer than you anticipate. An octave guitar solo comes in

after the second chorus. Listen carefully to the backing vocals, the highest line of which sound as though they have been electronically pitch-shifted. Technology has progressed but such effects can't entirely remove the 'Chipmunk' effect. This can be heard on the fade-out as the other voices are pulled away, and suggests perhaps the band thought it was funny enough to have as a little joke ending.

PEACEKEEPER
(Lindsey Buckingham)

ANOTHER single lifted from the album, and like the title-track another mid-tempo gentle rocker in a minor key. This is one of the stronger melodies, with good harmonies from Nicks. There's a nice Spanish guitar-style 'tremolando' figure after the second chorus which leads into several bars of Buckingham's trademark splintered arpeggios. The lilting last choruses have Buckingham adding another vocal melody line in contrast to the main one, and at the same time layering a high lead guitar solo with some classic rock/blues licks. Another engimatic lyric since a peacekeeper might operate in the personal or the political sphere.

COME
(Lindsey Buckingham/ Neale Heywood)

THE SONG'S writer told *Guitar World* (June 2003), "It's all based on the idea of trying to break vocal lines down into facets, the same way Cubism breaks down a visual line. Each part of each vocal line was sung separately and recorded on a separate track. Then each track was processed a little differently. So one part of the line might have a flangy effect, and the next part a 'wet' reverb. So you're making the whole thing more artificial, in the way Cubism does, but it gives you a whole spatial world."

'Come' is an effective exercise in dynamics harnessed to a sardonic lyric. There's an atmospheric intro in stereo, with pulsating stereo guitars, and voices left right and centre. You have to listen to this on headphones to appreciate the mix. Verse two brings minimal bass drum work to mark the bars. At about 1:30 the track explodes with heavy drums, electric guitar and a distorted lead vocal, like something that Jack White [of The White Stripes] might have produced, echoed to one side and distorted. It has an effective traditional guitar solo with held bends and repeat licks. Stabs of organ help out underneath. This track is maybe a bit on the long side at almost six minutes but is an obvious contender for live performance.

SMILE AT YOU
(Stevie Nicks)

THIS HAS a filigree texture of acoustic guitar arpeggios ticking away like clocks. It's a song of lost love and personal recrimination, as Nicks considers she should have turned and run away from the situation described. At about 2:15 you can hear the spectral trace of reverse reverb on her voice (the reverb precedes the sound that is supposed to have made it, creating a ghostly 'sucking' noise). The tone of the acoustic guitar heard towards the end is exactly that which Buckingham played on *Rumours* – something of a signature tone, so presumably it was the same instrument. The rhythm section are subtle on this but John McVie cuts loose a bit with the bass line.

RUNNING THROUGH THE GARDEN
(Lyrics: Stevie Nicks; music: Gary Nicholson/Ray Kennedy)

WRITTEN around 1985, this song relates to Nathaniel Hawthorne's short story 'Rappacini's Daughter'. Musically in 'Rhiannon' territory and lyrically, this song finds Nicks in full sub-Tennysonian flowers, garden and a fatal woman mode. A quiet opening verse leads to an uptempo second verse, which in turn steps up into a 'rock chick' chorus with a monotonous melody.

The chorus phrases are echoed by backing vocals. Buckingham gets in a fidgety solo after the second chorus. There's a descending synth figure toward the end. The second squealing solo played very high livens up the coda. It is easy to imagine this being extended live.

SILVER GIRL
(Stevie Nicks)

LYRICALLY, a companion piece to the earlier 'Miranda', as it features another one of Nicks' enigmatic female characters, 'a wild adventurer' who is 'sometimes just an actress'. Perhaps it's a veiled self-portrait... but we'll never really know, apparently. Certainly, if one of these buttoned you at a party you'd be reaching for your coat and calling a taxi. Speaking to *The Times* (April 2003), Nicks said it is partly about Sheryl Crow but also herself: "It's an ode to a lady rock star who's always on the road and has a very hard time having relationships and settling down. So it's totally about me. Being a female rock star is great... but every relationship I've ever had has been destroyed by this business."

Musically, it's another outing for the charming 'tremolo' guitar effect. A languid, midtempo ballad close to the atmosphere of 'Dreams' in which Buckingham's guitar is well-judged for the context.

STEAL YOUR HEART AWAY
(Lindsey Buckingham)

STARTS OFF like a Traveling Wilburys song – you almost can hear Jeff Lynne coming in on vocals. The lyric is excessively generalized; its blandness doesn't evoke anything in particular. Buckingham sings lead on this ballad. The first verse is followed by a good acoustic guitar break. The rhythm section are impressively metronomic on this fairly classic Mac vibe that would sound good on the radio. Am I right in thinking I can hear Christine McVie on the backing vocals on the right? That's a magic moment for the coda.

BLEED TO LOVE HER
(Lindsey Buckingham)

THIS SONG was first heard as a live recording on 1997's *The Dance*. It's a finger-picked guitar song about love that's desired but unable to be followed up. This is one of the album's strongest choruses with a female voice on the backing on the left. The pointed lyric is delivered by vocals that get progressively dense in texture and cover all the frequencies. Buckingham sounds in good voice. On the coda there's guitar through a volume pedal, another Mac trademark from 'Dreams'. The only drawback is that it just rambles a bit toward the end. It feels under-composed in that it would be stronger with another section or chord in this last bit to add interest.

EVERYBODY FINDS OUT
(Lyrics: Stevie Nicks; music: Rick Nowels)

THE PRODUCTION starts out emasculated as though it's coming through a radio speaker (a mixing technique featured again at about 2:40). This uptempo song has a clearer-cut lyric than some of the tracks but an uninteresting melody replete with Nicks' favourite notes and descending phrases. The lyric is about the cost of a secret affair and the judgement of others. The title is bleakly realistic. Buckingham's vocal brings a needed urgency to the chorus. At 3:00 there are a few synth phrases which come as quite a surprise. McVie supplies a grooving bass line within the constraints of the sequence. The 'strings' really take over before the final fade, punctuated by some effective drum rolls from Fleetwood.

DESTINY RULES
(Stevie Nicks)

THIS BEGINS with the type of blues acoustic riff which has already been used on the album and therefore doesn't sound as effective here. The song lifts with the dramatic entry by the rhythm section. The chorus has a typical Mac IV-V chord change, like 'Dreams' taken at a business-like, brisk pace. This song repeats a verse lyric from 'Illume'. The coda brings in a new four-chord progression and guitar-phrase at 3:30 which is easily the best moment of the song (this is what the end of 'Bleed To Love Her' needed) and an unexpected inspiration.

SAY GOODBYE
(Lindsey Buckingham)

SAY YOU WILL ends with a touching pair of songs that offer themselves for interpretation as personal statements between two of the protagonists in rock's longest-running soap opera. This song was written in 1997 or thereabouts. Buckingham goes at it with a lateral movement. This has fast fingerpicking, a Burt Bacharach major 7th, and a melody in which the words are crammed into the available space. The hurried nature of it suggests a desire to be indirect. The sadness of the underlying emotion is off-set by the speed of the song and its abrupt ending. Fans who like this might want to check out UK band Gene, because although faster than their material there's something about the melody that's reminiscent of that band.

The most successful line-up of the long-lived band, clockwise from top left: Mick Fleetwood, Christine McVie, Lindsay Buckingham, Steve Nicks and John McVie. *(LFI)*

Mirage (1982)

Steve Nicks on stage. *(LFI)*

Tango In The Night (1987)

Left to right: Christine McVie, Buckingham, Nicks,
John McVie and Fleetwood. *(LFI)*

Steve Nicks in 1987. *(LFI)*

The 1987 Fleetwood Mac line-up with guitarists Rick Vito and
Billy Burnette having replaced Lindsey Buckingham, left to right: Vito,
Christine McVie, Mick Fleetwood, Stevie Nicks, Burnette and John McVie. *(LFI)*

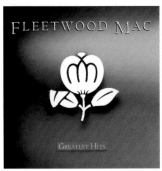

Greatest Hits (1988)

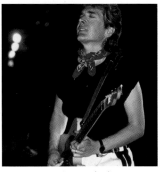

Rick Vito. *(LFI)*

Behind The Mask (1990)

Christine McVie and Stevie Nicks. *(LFI)*

Time (1995)

The Dance (1997)

Mick Fleetwood and Stevie Nicks on stage in 1997. *(LFI)*

The reformed group pose backstage before a show at the Meadowlands Arena, New Jersey, September 1997, left to right: Mick Fleetwood, Stevie Nicks, John and Christine McVie and Lindsey Buckingham. *(LFI)*

At the Brits, February 1998, collecting their award for Outstanding Contribution to British Music, left to right: John Mcvie, Lindsey Buckingham, Christine McVie, Stevie Nicks and Mick Fleetwood. *(LFI)*

John McVie and Stevie Nicks on stage at Birmingham NEC, November, 2003. *(LFI)*

Fleetwood Mac performing on *The Today Show*, New York, April 18, 2003, clockwise from top left: Stevie Nicks, Mick Fleetwood, John McVie and Lindsey Buckingham. *(LFI)*

GOODBYE BABY
(Stevie Nicks)

THE ALBUM is finished off with this ballad which sounds like an obvious last encore before the crowds extinguish their pocket lighters for the final time. This is one of Nicks' better vocals if only because the initial fragility sounds genuine. The continual pitter-patter of high guitars, distant strings, subdued keyboards, and a low-level bass drone, bring the album to a quiet close.

LIVE ALBUMS

London Live '68

Thunderbolt CD TB 1.038 (1984)

TRACKS: 'Got To Move', 'I Held My Baby Last Night', 'My Baby's Sweet', 'My Baby's A Good 'Un', 'Don't Know Which Way To Go', 'Buzz Me', 'The Dream', 'The World Keeps On Turning', 'How Blue Can You Get', 'Bleeding Heart'.

R ECORDED BY THE LINE-UP THAT PLAYED THE WINDSOR BLUES AND JAZZ FESTIVAL in the summer of 1967, so John McVie was not on bass. The CD says it was recorded live in London in 1968, though some reviewers state it is 15 August 1967, two days after the Windsor debut. Bob Brunning's book says that the band's next gig after Windsor was at the Marquee on 15 September. This material has been frequently re-issued so when purchasing check the track-listing carefully for a match. Two examples are *The Masters* (Eagle, 1998) and *Live!* (Columbia River Ent. 1999).

Cerulean

Music Galore HAI 300 (1984)

TRACKS: 'Madison Blues', 'Sandy Mary', 'Stranger Blues', 'Great Balls Of Fire', 'Jenny Jenny', 'Got To Move', 'Oh Baby', 'Teenage Darling', 'Loving Kind', 'Tutti Frutti', 'Rattlesnake Shake,' 'Keep A Knocking', 'Red Hot Mama', 'Green Manalishi'

T HE SLEEVE NOTES EXPLAIN THAT THESE TAPES OF THE 1969 BOSTON SHOW when the band were on their second US tour were intended for release by Fleetwood Mac as a live album in the early Seventies but the project was abandoned when the band split. This package claims that this is the first issue of these recordings. *Cerulean* captures that part of the set where the band dressed in gold lame suits to masquerade as 'Earl Vince & The Valiants', Spencer's pastiche of Fifties rock'n'roll. The missing numbers in the set are on the next item, presumably released at the same time.

Fleetwood Mac
Live In Boston

HA1 107; Cassette HAC 107

Boston Live

Castle CLA CD 152 (1989)

TRACKS: 'Oh Well', 'Like It This Way', 'World In Harmony', 'Only You', 'Black Magic Woman', 'Jumping At Shadows', 'Can't Hold On'

THIS COLLECTION OF LIVE TRACKS FIRST APPEARED ON MUSIC GALORE IN 1984. The recording is from the Boston Tea Party gig.

Peter Green's
Fleetwood Mac Live At
The Marquee

Receiver RR CD 157 (1992)

TRACKS: 'Talk To Me Baby', 'I Held My Baby Last Night', 'My Baby's Sweet', 'Looking For Somebody', 'Evil Woman Blues', 'Got To Move', 'No Place To Go', 'Watch Out For Me Woman', 'Mighty Long Tree', 'Dust My Blues', 'I Need You, Come On Home To Me', 'Shake Your Moneymaker'

THE BAND CAUGHT VERY EARLY IN THEIR CAREER. THE SOUND QUALITY ISN'T UP to much, but the historical value is undeniable. Reissued on the Cleopatra label in 1999 and on Sanctuary in 2001.

Madison Blues Live

Castle MBSCD 431 /1 (1994)

TRACKS: 'Black Magic Woman', 'Can't Hold On', 'Got To Move', 'Green Manalishi', 'Like It This Way', 'Madison Blues', 'Oh Well', 'Only You', 'Red Hot Mama', 'Sandy Mary', 'Teenage Darling', 'World In Harmony'

THE SLEEVE GIVES NO DETAILS ABOUT THE RECORDING DATE. THIS IS ONE of a number of issues of some of *Live In Boston*. There are fine, raw versions of 'Black Magic Woman' and 'Green Manalishi'. See also *Fleetwood Mac The Blues Years* (PLS CD 198).

Live At The BBC

Castle Communications EDF CD 297 (1995)

CD 1: 'Rattleshake Shake', 'Sandy Mary', 'Believe My Time Ain't Long', 'Although The Sun Is Shining', 'Only You', 'You Never Know What You're Missing', 'Oh Well', 'Can't Believe You Want To Leave', 'Jenny Lee', 'Heavenly', 'When Will I Be Loved', 'When I See My Baby', 'Buddy's Song', 'Honey Hush', 'Preachin'', 'Jumping At Shadows', 'Preachin' Blues', 'Need Your Love So Bad'

CD 2: 'Long Grey Mare', 'Sweet Home Chicago', 'Baby Please Set A Date', 'Blues With A Feeling', 'Stop Messing Around', 'Tallahassie Lassie', 'Hang On To A Dream', 'Linda', 'Mean Mistreating Mama', 'World Keeps Turning', 'I Can't Hold Out', 'Early Morning Come', 'Albatross', 'Looking For Somebody', 'A Fool No More', 'Got To Move', 'Like Crying Like Dying', 'Man Of The World'

WHEN THIS DOUBLE SET APPEARED IN 1995 FANS OF THE ORIGINAL FLEETWOOD Mac probably couldn't believe their luck. No less than 35 radio performances on this album capture something of the power of the band in its triple guitar line-up. It must be said that the Mac seemed always able to discipline the possibilities of chaos inherent in having three guitarists (contrast the imploding Beck/Page version of The Yardbirds - a case of this band ain't big enough for the two of us, let alone three). The material is extremely varied. Green leads some powerful renditions of classic tracks like 'Rattleshake Shake' and 'Oh Well'. Danny Kirwan is featured on plaintive versions of his lighter material like 'Although The Sun Is Shining'. Jeremy Spencer does Elmore James, Elvis ('You Never Know What You're Missing'), the Everly Brothers, Johnny Burnette and the Rock and Roll Trio, and Buddy Holly ('Buddy's Song').

The recordings were made largely in mono at the BBC in 1969 and 1970. The sleeve provides interesting notes and pictures. From it we learn that *Sandy Mary* would have been the title of the follow-up to *Then Play On* had the band not split. There are blues covers of songs by Robert Johnson, Duster Bennett, Fats Domino, Little Willie John amongst others. Though it demonstrates the band's breadth, there's too much joke material for the band to focus. They lacked the ruthlessness to pursue their own musical vision. There's a sense of talent here being squandered - especially Green's. It comes as a relief to get to the end of disc one and hear Green's lead guitar take over once more on 'Preachin' Blues'. The version on disc 1 of 'Need Your Love So Bad' is not listed on the CD cover. The sound quality on this track is noticeably inferior to the rest of the album.

Shrine '69

Rykodisc 1999

TRACKS: 'Tune Up', 'If You Be My Baby', 'Something Inside Of Me', 'My Baby's Sweet', 'Albatross', 'Before The Beginning', 'Rollin' Man', 'Lemon Squeezer', 'Need Your Love So Bad', 'Great Balls Of Fire'

THIS CONCERT IS EDITED DOWN TO FIT ON A SINGLE DISC. IT HAS POOR SOUND but some consider the performance itself excellent. Includes a live version of 'Before The Beginning'.

Boston Blues

Recall SMDCD274 (2000)

CD 1: 'Black Magic Woman', 'Like It This Way', 'Oh Well', 'Jumping At Shadows', 'Stranger Blues', 'Oh Baby', 'Got To Move', 'Rattlesnake Shake'

CD 2: 'World In Harmony', 'Sandy Mary', 'Loving Kind', 'Only You', 'Red Hot Mama', 'I Can't Hold Out Much Longer', 'Green Manalishi', 'Encore Jam'

ANOTHER version of the Boston gigs.

Live In Boston
Remastered Vol 1

Snapper Classics SDPCD122 (2003)

TRACKS: 'Black Magic Woman', 'Jumping At Shadows', 'Like It This Way', 'Only You', 'Rattlesnake Shake', 'I Can't Hold On Much Longer', 'Got To Move', 'Green Manalishi'

Live In Boston
Remastered Vol 2

Snapper Classics SDPCD556 (2003)

TRACKS: 'World In Harmony', 'Oh Well', 'Rattlesnake Shake', 'Stranger Blues', 'Red Hot Mama', 'Teenage Darling', 'Keep-a-Knocking', 'Jenny Jenny', 'Encore Jam'

Live In Boston
Remastered Vol 3

Snapper Classics SDPCD130 (2003)

TRACKS: 'Jumping At Shadows', 'Sandy Mary', 'If You Let Me Love You', 'Loving Kind', 'Coming Your Way', 'Madison Blues', 'Got To Move', 'The Sun Is Shining', 'Oh Baby', 'Tiger', 'Great Balls Of Fire', 'Tutti Frutti', 'On We Jam'

THE MUCH-ISSUED BOSTON RECORDINGS GET THE REMASTERING TREATMENT. These were also issued in 1999 as a three-CD box-set limited to 10,000 by Snapper Music.

Live

US Warner Bros 3500 December 1980; UK Warner Bros K 66097
December 1980; US CD Warner Bros 3500 2;
UK CD Warner Bros 927410 2

TRACKS: 'Monday Morning', 'Say You Love Me', 'Dreams', 'Oh Well', 'Over and Over', 'Sara', 'Not That Funny', 'Never Going Back Again', 'Landslide', 'Fireflies', 'Over My Head', 'Rhiannon', 'Don't Let Me Down Again', 'One More Night', 'Go Your Own Way', 'Don't Stop', 'I'm So Afraid', 'The Farmer's Daughter'

RECORDED ON THE *TUSK* WORLD TOUR OF 1979-80, THE INNER SLEEVES LIST ALL the dates and how many people they played to. Unlike most live doubles, this is a set where many of the songs actually improve on their originals. Numbers like 'Monday Morning', 'Over And Over' and 'Say You Love Me' which come over as a little underpowered on the studio albums are here given an extra kick and are all the better for it. 'Rhiannon' and 'I'm So Afraid' are more epic in performance and Nicks turns in a touching performance of 'Landslide' with a fine sense of dynamics. 'Dreams' and 'Don't Stop' were recorded at a Paris sound check. 'Fireflies', 'One More Night' and Brian Wilson's 'Farmer's Daughter' were recorded live at the Santa Monica Civic Auditorium 'for crew and friends'. Along with 'Don't Let Me Down Again', these tracks are previously unreleased. The sleeve carries the note 'To Brian: Thank you for The Farmer's Daughter, you're the greatest.' And so say all of us.

The Dance

CD Reprise 9362-46702-2 (1997)

TRACKS: 'The Chain', 'Dreams', 'Everywhere', 'Rhiannon', 'I'm So Afraid', 'Temporary One', 'Bleed To Love Her', 'Big Love', 'Landslide', 'Say You Love Me', 'My Little Demon', 'Silver Springs', 'You Make Loving Fun', 'Sweet Girl', 'Go Your Own Way', 'Tusk', 'Don't Stop'

IN MAY 1997, IN BURBANK, CALIFORNIA, FLEETWOOD MAC WAS ONCE MORE Buckingham, Nicks, McVie, McVie and Fleetwood. The classic line-up that had turned their relationship agonies into several of the Seventies best-selling platters were re-united for three nights playing before an ecstatic audience of Mac-o-philes. For the set the Mac drew on their Seventies and

Eighties back catalogue of greatest hits and spiced up the proceedings with some new songs. *The Dance* is the result, running at 79 minutes virtually a double album. The band's sound is filled out with additional keyboard and guitars, percussion and backing vocals. The presence of the USC Marching Band enables 'Tusk' to be performed.

The performances generally follow the arrangements of the studio performances. The renditions of old songs have more of a decorous weight about them if less attack. The guitar solo on 'You Make Loving Fun' is a bit sedate. 'Rhiannon' is another example of this. It enters disguised with a delicate piano intro and Nicks drawing out the tune. Then the guitar riff kicks in. There's no long solo on this take, which doesn't build up the steam of the Seventies live version. Some of the melodies have been 'shaved' of their top notes to match the slight drop in vocal range caused by the passing of the years, but the vocal harmonies on 'Dreams' are exquisite. 'I'm So Afraid' retains its neo-Gothic gloom and lumbering gait, while the solo shows how Buckingham was playing some Edge-like stuff before U2 were a twinkle in Bono's eye. Clearly for the band, the songs have taken on extra resonance with the passage of the years. This is especially felt on the *Rumours* material. One surprise track is a brilliant performance of 'Silver Springs' with a spirited middle eight and coda, where Nicks excels herself.

There are four new songs. 'Temporary One' (C. McVie/Quintela) is a typical uptempo Mac pop tune with some nice harmonies on the chorus. Lindsey Buckingham contributes 'Bleed To Love Her' which starts with finger-picked acoustic and becomes a medium-paced reflective tune. This song would get a studio release on 2003's *Say You Will*. 'My Little Demon' has a playful intro, alternating vocals with guitars and strange noises before it drives off in classic Mac groove, though it's not one of Buckingham's strongest melodies. Nicks offers 'Sweet Girl', a reflection on her life on the stage.

In 1997 I wrote that *The Dance* suggested that given a suitable creative effort there was no reason why this line-up shouldn't make another good studio album, which they did (albeit without Christine McVie) in 2003.

COMPILATION
ALBUMS

UNDER THE GUISE OF THEIR VARIOUS LINE-UPS, FLEETWOOD MAC HAVE been releasing music for almost thirty years. With 20 studio albums to their collective credit, that means a lot of music to sort through. So if a band deserved a compilation, it would be the Mac. However, they have recorded for a number of different labels so at times it has been problematic to assemble a compilation to cover all the line-ups and phases of their career. What follows is a guide to the compilation albums of both line-ups. They are mostly of the Peter Green period. Some of these are significant for collecting several important tracks that appeared only on singles during the close of the Sixties. Only two compilations - *The Chain* and the UK version of *The Very Best Of Fleetwood Mac* - has ventured into the phase between Green's departure and the coming of Nicks and Buckingham. The 1971 *Greatest Hits* has now been superseded by *The Best Of Peter Green's Fleetwood Mac* (2002) as the best introduction to Green's Fleetwood Mac, and the 1988 *Greatest Hits* gives way to *The Very Best Of Fleetwood Mac* (2002) for the *Rumours*-era band.

Box-sets

IF YOU WANT TO EXPLORE OUT-TAKES THE LANDMARK RELEASE IS *THE COMPLETE Blue Horizon* box-set (Sire/WEA 1999). These six CDs (99 tracks) include the albums *Fleetwood Mac, Mr Wonderful, The Pious Bird of Good Omen, Blues Jam in Chicago Vols 1* and *2*, and *The Original Fleetwood Mac*. But what you also get is studio banter, false starts and alternate takes interspersed. If you wish you could have been a fly on the wall when the band were recording this may be your taste. Otherwise you could programme the CD player to just play the official album tracks.

25 Years –
The Chain Box Set

CD 1: 'Paper Doll', 'Love Shines', 'Stand Back (Live)', 'Crystal', ' Isn't It Midnight', 'Big Love', 'Everywhere', 'Affairs Of The Heart', 'Heart Of Stone', 'Sara', 'That's All For Everyone', 'Over My Head', 'Little Lies', 'Eyes Of The World', 'Oh Diane', 'In The Back Of My Mind', 'Make Me A Mask'

CD 2: 'Save Me', 'Goodbye Angel ', 'Silver Springs', 'What Makes You Think You're The One', 'Think About Me', 'Gypsy', 'You Make Loving Fun', 'Second Hand News', 'Love In Store', 'The Chain', ' Teen Beat', 'Dreams', 'Only Over You', 'I'm So Afraid', 'Love Is Dangerous', 'Gold Dust Woman', 'Not That Funny'

CD 3: 'Warm Ways', 'Say You Love Me', 'Don't Stop', 'Rhiannon', 'Walk A Thin Line', 'Storms', 'Go Your Own Way', 'Sisters Of The Moon', 'Monday Morning', 'Landslide', 'Hypnotized', 'Lay It All Down', 'Angel', 'Beautiful Child', 'Brown Eyes', 'Save Me A Place', ' Tusk', 'Never Going Back Again', 'Songbird'

CD 4: 'I Believe My Time Ain't Long', 'Need Your Love So Bad', 'Rattlesnake Shake', 'Oh Well, Part 1', 'Stop Messin' Around', 'Green Manalishi', 'Albatross', 'Man Of The World ', 'Love That Burns', 'Black Magic Woman', 'Watch Out', 'String-A-Long', 'Station Man', 'Did You Ever Love Me', 'Sentimental Lady', 'Come A Little Bit Closer', 'Heroes Are Hard To Find', 'Trinity', 'Why'

THIS BOX-SET DEVOTES THREE CDs TO THE *RUMOURS* BAND AND THE FOURTH to earlier line-ups. A cut-down two-CD version with the same title was also released (see below).

Fleetwood Mac Greatest Hits

US Not Released; UK CBS 69011 November 1971
Reissues: UK CBS 460704 1 (1988), UK CD CBS 460704 2

TRACKS: 'The Green Manalishi (With The Two-Pronged Crown)', 'Oh Well Part 1', 'Oh Well Part 2', 'Shake Your Moneymaker', 'Dragonfly', 'Black Magic Woman', 'Albatross', 'Man Of The World', 'Stop Messin' Round', 'Love That Burns'

IN 1971 THIS MADE A REASONABLE JOB OF PUTTING TOGETHER A 'BEST OF' FOR the band, pulling in the hit singles and salting it all with a few famous album tracks. It shows the band's wonderful moments of imagination and doesn't allow Jeremy Spencer off the leash. It has now been superseded by the better-value *The Best of Peter Green's Fleetwood Mac* (2002).

All the tracks bar three have already been discussed. So here we just need to stop and enjoy the following:

THE GREEN MANALISHI (WITH THE TWO-PRONGED CROWN)
(P.A.Green)

WAS THERE ever such a glorious swan-song as this? 'Manalishi' was Peter Green's last great recording with the band and one of his 'magic quartet' (with 'Albatross', 'Man Of The World', 'Oh Well'). This dates to April 1970, with Green pressing into service not only his trusty '59 Les Paul but also his Fender Bass VI. The song was based on a nightmare he had. The Green Manalishi is a personification of the seductive power of money - the money that rock stardom was bringing to him and which Green felt was cutting him off from reality. The Green Manalishi is "the wad of notes", Green told *Guitar* magazine (January 1997). "The devil is green and he was after me. It ended up big, a heavy thing. It was heavy chords and big African drums and it was very black when I woke up... I found I was writing this song... Fear, inspiration is what it was, but it was that tribal ancient Hebrew thing I was going for. Ancient music." The song also expressed something of the Munich experience and its aftermath.

To get a massive sound, speaker cabs were placed in the underground car park at De Lane Lea studios. Close and distance miking was used on the speakers to get a very original guitar sound. 'Green Manalishi' starts with a throbbing E minor chord and after a pause to build up the tension, Green laconically delivers the first line of the song, which is followed by a heavy E G A blues-type chord riff. Each verse is rounded off by a twisted single note riff that spirals around and ends on an F. There's another riff sequence where thirds are moved down over an E pedal note. With a superb sense of dynamics, the third verse ends with a chord dying away before a single note run twists into the extended coda. Here Green does his own take on Howlin' Wolf, with a series of eerie wordless cries heavy with reverb. Listen carefully to this section and in the back of the pounding guitars you'll hear him play an extended solo reminiscent of Jimmy Page at his most expressive.

DRAGONFLY
(D.Kirwan/W.H.Davies)

THIS IS A slow shuffling minor key instrumental with wonderfully textured guitar playing. It has shimmering chords and the tune coming down in octaves. Kirwan harmonizing with himself as he sings the words (presumably written by the poet W.H.Davies), full of evocative images about a dragonfly in a garden. Kirwan plays some fine lead, and the rhythm section turn in a sensitive performance perfect for the track. Watch out for the sudden

unexpected chord change just seconds before the end. This is far and away the best thing which Kirwan ever wrote.

MAN OF THE WORLD
(P.A.Green)

DON'T YOU laugh when you hear it?," Green asked his Guitar. interviewer, stating he thought the lyrics were hammy, though a real heartache lies behind it. On this one, I'm afraid the jury is unanimously against its composer's assessment. Recorded in early January 1969 in New York, 'Man Of The World' is one of the most poignant slices of soul-baring ever released by a rock band. It uses a pretty D-A-G minor chord sequence, while Green muses about the meaning of success, of having travelled around the world, and the loss of love. There is a moment of anguish when his voice soars into the ether as he cries, "I just wish that I'd never been born". After a brief instrumental break, the band suddenly explode into an F# minor middle eight with some superb lead fills. Within a few seconds it all dies away again. Conceding nothing to the demands of radio, Green appends a final coda of rolled chords and ends on a delicate harmonic.

Can you imagine a song like this going top three now? Scary, huh?

Vintage Years

Sire Sash 3706-2; US Release March 1971; CBS 88227 UK Release 1977

TRACKS: 'Black Magic Woman', 'Coming Home', 'Rambling Pony', 'Something Inside Of Me', 'Dust My Broom', 'The Sun Is Shining', 'Albatross', 'Just The Blues', 'Evening Boogie', 'The Big Boat', 'Jigsaw Puzzle Blues', 'I've Lost My Baby', 'Doctor Brown', 'Need Your Love So Bad', 'Looking For Somebody', 'Need Your Love Tonight', 'Shake Your Moneymaker', 'Man Of The World', 'Stop Messin' Round', 'Rollin' Man', 'Love That Burns', 'If You Be My Baby', 'Lazy Poker Blues', 'Trying So Hard To Forget'

REISSUED AS HISTORY OF *FLEETWOOD MAC: VINTAGE YEARS* DOUBLE-ALBUM CBS 22122 in 1990. A reasonable selection but notice the absence of 'Oh Well', 'Dragonfly' and 'Green Manalishi'.

Albatross

(Fleetwood Mac And Christine Perfect)

CBS 31569 Released August 1977; CD Columbia CD 31569 Released February 1991.

TRACKS: 'Albatross', 'Rambling Pony', 'I Believe My Time Ain't Long', 'Doctor Brown', 'Stop Messin' Round', 'Love That Burns', 'Jigsaw Puzzle Blues', 'Need Your Love Tonight'

CHRISTINE PERFECT: 'I'd Rather Go Blind', 'Crazy 'Bout You Baby', 'And That's Saying A Lot', 'I'm On My Way', 'No Road Is The Right Road', 'Let Me Go (Leave Me Alone)', 'I'm Too Far Gone To Turn Around', 'When You Say'

THIS COMPRISES TRACKS BY FLEETWOOD MAC AND TRACKS TAKEN FROM THE album *Christine Perfect* (1970).

Man Of The World

Reprise Rep 44138; UK Only, 1978.

TRACKS: 'Oh Well', 'Dragonfly', 'Rattlesnake Shake', 'World In Harmony', 'The Green Manalishi', 'Searching For Madge', 'Before The Beginning', 'The Purple Dancer', 'Fighting For Madge', 'Coming Your Way'

CHIEFLY NOTABLE FOR THE RARE 'THE PURPLE DANCER' AND FOR SELECTING THE brilliant 'Before The Beginning'.

Black Magic Woman

CBS LP 31798; Released February 1980

TRACKS: 'Black Magic Woman', 'Coming Home', 'Lazy Poker Blues', 'Something Inside Of Me', 'Evenin' Boogie', 'If You Be My Baby', 'Without You', 'Rockin' Boogie', 'Need Your Love So Bad', 'Rollin' Man', 'Dust My Broom', 'I've Lost My Baby', 'Big Boat', 'Shake Your Moneymaker', 'Sun Is Shining', 'Last Night'

THIS SELECTION PUT THE EMPHASIS ON GREEN-ERA BLUES. NOTICE THE single hits are missing.

Fleetwood Mac: The Collection

Castle CCSCD 157; Released July 1987; Vinyl Double CCSLP 157; Cassette CCSMC 157

TRACKS: 'Shake Your Moneymaker ', 'Long Grey Mare', 'I Loved Another Woman', 'Got To Move ', 'World Keep On Turning', 'Black Magic Woman ', 'Need Your Love So Bad', 'Doctor Brown', 'Need Your Love Tonight', 'Love That Burns', 'Lazy Poker Blues', 'Dust My Broom', 'Drifting', 'Fleetwood Mac', 'Love That Woman', 'I've Lost My Baby', 'Man Of The World', 'Someone's Gonna Get Their Head Kicked In Tonight', 'Watch Out', 'Homework', 'Rockin' Boogie', 'Jigsaw Puzzle Blues', 'Albatross'

THIS 65 MINUTE 20-TRACK SELECTION OF THE GREEN ERA BAND PUTS THE emphasis on the blues. 'Man Of The World' is present with its B-side 'Someone's Gonna Get Their Head Kicked In Tonight' but 'Oh Well' and 'Green Manalishi' are missing.

Greatest Hits

US Warner Bros 25801-1; November 1988; UK Warner Bros WX 221 November 1988; US CD Warner Bros 25838 2 (1988) With Three Extra - You Make Loving Fun', 'Big Love', 'Over My Head. UK CD Warner Bros 925838 -2 (1988) With Four Extra Tracks As US Plus 'Oh Diane'

TRACKS: 'Rhiannon', 'Don't Stop', 'Go Your Own Way', 'Hold Me', 'Everywhere', 'Gypsy', 'As Long As You Follow', 'Say You Love Me', 'Dreams', 'Little Lies', 'Sara', 'Tusk', 'No Questions Asked'

IF YOU DIDN'T HAVE ANY OF THE MID-SEVENTIES FLEETWOOD MAC, THEN THIS was a reasonable summary of that line-up's music when it was released. It makes a startling contrast with the *Greatest Hits* (1971) of the Peter Green era. Nothing here can quite match the best tracks on that record, but judged against their Seventies contemporaries, the later Fleetwood Mac's best songs stand up pretty well. Now superseded by *The Very Best of Fleetwood Mac* (2002)

All the tracks bar two have been discussed elsewhere, so we must just have a look at two previously unreleased numbers:

AS LONG AS YOU FOLLOW
(C. McVie)

THIS HAS A lovely tumbling guitar figure over a lushly orchestrated introduction. This guitar figure comes back throughout the track. Christine takes the lead on this slow-ish ballad, supported by Nicks and Buckingham on the chorus harmonies. The second verse has little flourishes of Spanish guitar. This is a very full arrangement. There's a good lead break in the middle which ends with a couple of phrases out of Amos Garrett's 'Midnight At The Oasis' phrase-book. A very attractive track that holds its own in the somewhat elevated company of the hits. In November 1988 this was released as a single.

NO QUESTIONS ASKED
(Nicks)

A SPRIGHTLY bright guitar figure and a big thumping guitar sound get this track going. Stevie

Nicks takes the vocal addressing the man in her mind. Sonically, this track occupies quite a bit of elbow-room. The best bit is toward the end, where the guitars repeat their attractive, woody-sounding arpeggio. It's okay but isn't up to the standard of 'As Long As You Follow'.

Looking Back At Fleetwood Mac

Pickwick SHM 3268; CD PWK S533; UK Only 1989

TRACKS: 'Albatross', 'Looking For Somebody', 'My Baby's Good To Me', 'I Loved Another Woman', 'If You Be Baby', 'Without You', 'Jigsaw Puzzle Blues', 'Black Magic Woman', 'Need Your Love So Bad', 'Love That Burns', 'My Heart Beats Like A Hammer', 'I Believe My Time Ain't Long', 'Shake Your Moneymaker', 'World Keeps On Turning', 'Stop Messin' Round', 'Coming Home'

THE Green line-up once more.

The Original Fleetwood Mac: The Blues Years

Essential ESBCD 138; Vinyl ESBLP 138; CD ESBCD 138; Released February 1991

TRACKS: 'My Heart Beat Like A Hammer', 'Merry Go Round', 'Long Grey Mare', 'Hellhound On My Trail', 'Shake Your Moneymaker', 'Looking For Somebody', 'No Place To Go', 'My Baby's Good To Me', 'I Loved Another Woman', 'Cold Black Night', 'World Keep On Turning', 'Got To Move', 'Stop Messin' Round', 'Coming Home', 'Rollin' Man', 'Dust My Broom', 'Love That Burns', 'Doctor Brown', 'Need Your Love Tonight', 'If You Be My Baby', 'Evenin' Boogie', 'Lazy Poker Blues', 'I've Lost My Baby', 'Trying So Hard To Forget', 'I Believe My Time Ain't Long', 'Ramblin' Pony', 'Black Magic Woman', 'Sun Is Shining', 'Need Your Love So Bad', 'Albatross', 'Jigsaw Puzzle Blues', 'Man Of The World', 'Someone's Gonna Get Their Head Kicked In

Tonight', 'Watch Out', 'Worried Dream', 'Fleetwood Mac', 'First Train Home', 'Drifting', 'Mean Old Fireman', 'Allow Me One More Show', ' Just The Blues', 'Big Boat', 'I'd Rather Go Blind', 'Watch Out (2nd version)', 'Homework', 'I Can't Hold Out', 'Like It This Way', 'Last Night', 'I'm Worried', 'Worlds In A Tangle'

THREE CD SET THAT INCLUDES THE BAND'S FIRST TWO ALBUMS, VARIOUS HIT singles, 7 cuts from the blues jam at Chicago. Plus Chicken Shack's version of Etta James''I'd Rather Go Blind' on which Christine Perfect sang lead. Strong on the blues. Notice the absence of 'Oh Well' and 'Green Manalishi'.

The Chain

Warner Bros 9362-45188-2; Released 1992

TRACKS: 'Paper Doll', 'Love Shines', 'Love In Store', 'Goodbye Angel', 'Heart Of Stone', 'Silver Springs', 'Oh Diane', 'Big Love', 'Rhiannon', 'Crystal', 'The Chain', 'Over My Head', 'Dreams', 'Go Your Own Way', 'Sara', 'Hold Me', 'Gypsy', 'Make Me A Mask', 'Don't Stop', 'Everywhere', 'Tusk', 'Not That Funny', 'Beautiful Child', 'Teen Beat', 'Need Your Love So Bad', 'Did You Ever Leave Me', 'Oh Well Part 1', 'I Believe My Time Ain't Long', 'Bermuda Triangle', 'Why', 'Station Man', 'Albatross', 'Black Magic Woman', 'Stop Messin' Round', 'Trinity', 'Heroes Are Hard To Find', 'Green Manalishi'

AN INTERESTING TWO-CD GREATEST HITS CUT DOWN FROM THE FOUR-CD BOX-set, from the Green era through *Rumours* and up to the Nineties. This was the first compilation to cover the whole history of the band and includes some rare tracks. No room for 'Oh Well' or 'Man Of The World'.

Like It This Way

Pickwick Elite CD 008CD; Mc 008MC; Released May 1991

TRACKS: 'Lazy Poker Blues', 'Something Inside Of Me ', 'Evenin' Boogie', 'Rockin' Boogie', 'Dust My Broom', 'Rollin' Man', 'Merry Go Round', 'Hellhound On My Trail', 'Last Night', 'Need Your Love Tonight', 'Rambling Pony', 'I Can't Hold Out', 'Like It This Way', 'Homework', 'Cold Black Night', 'Big Boat', 'Just The Blues', 'Dragonfly', 'Trying So Hard To Forget'

MORE EARLY FLEETWOOD MAC BLUES-BASED MATERIAL, SPICED UP with 'Dragonfly'.

The Vaudeville Years
Fleetwood Mac 1968-70

Vol.1

Receiver Records RDPCD (1998)

CD 1: 'Intro/Lazy Poker Blues', 'My Baby's Sweeter', 'Love That Burns', 'Talk To Me Baby', 'Every Day I Have The Blues, Pt1', 'Jeremy's Contribution To Doo-wop', 'Every Day I Have The Blues, Pt 2', 'Death Bells', '(Watch Out For Yourself) Mr.Jones', 'Man Of Action', 'Do You Give A Damn For Me', 'Man of the World', 'Like It This Way', 'Blues In B Flat Minor', 'Someone's Gonna Get Their Head Kicked In Tonight', 'Although The Sun Is Shining', 'Showbiz Blues'

CD 2: 'Underway', 'Madge Sessions 1-3', 'Madge Sessions (Pt2)', '(That's What) I Want To Know', 'Oh Well', 'Love It Seems', 'Mighty Cold', 'Fast Talking Woman Blues', 'Tell Me From The Start', 'October Jam (Pt1)', 'October Jam (Pt2)', 'Green Manalishi (With The Two-Pronged Crown)', 'World In Harmony', 'Farewell'

Show-Biz Blues
Fleetwood Mac 1968-70

Vol.2

Receiver Records RDPCD 15z (2001)

CD 1: 'Soul Dressing', 'If You Want To Be Happy', 'Outrage', 'The Sun Is Shining', 'Don't Be Cruel', 'I'm So Lonely And Blues', 'How Blue Can You Get?', 'My Baby's Sweeter', 'Long Grey Mare', 'Buzz Me Baby', 'Mind Of My Own', 'I Have To Laugh', 'You're The One', 'Do You Give A Damn For Me', 'Him and Me', 'Show-Biz Blues', 'Fast Talkin' Woman Blues', 'World In Harmony', 'Leaving Town Blues

CD 2: 'Black Magic Woman', 'Jumpin' At Shadows', 'Rattlesnake Shake-Underway', 'Stranger Blues', 'World In Harmony', 'Tiger', 'The Green Manalishi (with the Two Prong Crown)', 'Coming Your Way', 'Great Balls Of Fire', 'Twist and Shout'

FOUR CDs OF MOSTLY UNISSUED VERSIONS, UNISSUED INSTRUMENTALS, unissued songs, unissued studio versions, and the odd demo, with several alternative takes of previously released songs. *Vaudeville*'s first CD features Jeremy Spencer's skit character Milton Schlitz. CD2 features out-takes for the *Then Play On* album. Tracks 1-2 on *Showbiz Blues CD2* are unissued versions from the first night of the Boston concerts on Feb 5, 1970. The remaining tracks on CD2 are a London concert from 1970. Tracks 1-3 onCD1 ofVol 2 feature Peter Bardens on keys, Green, David Ambrose bass and Mick Fleetwood in 1966. Tracks 4-10 are the Spencer/Green/McVie/Fleetwood line-up.

Jumpin' At Shadows: The Blues Years

Indigo', 'Sanctuary IGOXDCD 2507 (2002)

CD 1: 'Black Magic Woman' [live], 'Jumpin'At Shadows' [live], 'Oh Well' [live], 'Ride With Your Daddy Tonight', 'Do You Give A Damn For Me?', 'Love That Burns', 'World In Harmony', 'Long Grey Mare', 'Talk To Me Baby', 'Fast Talking Woman Blues', 'Man Of The World' [early version], 'If You Let Me Love You', 'My Baby's Sweeter', 'Like It This Way', 'The Madge Sessions No.2', 'Lazy Poker Blues', 'I Have To Laugh', 'The Green Manalishi'

CD 2: 'Man Of The World' [single version], 'Showbiz Blues', 'Buzz Me Baby', 'Blues In B Flat Minor', 'It Takes Time', 'Leaving Town Blues', 'The Sun Is Shining', 'Uranus', 'Mind Of My Own', 'How Blue Can You Get?', 'Trying So Hard To Forget', 'Two Harps', 'Thinking About A Woman', 'Kind Hearted Woman', 'Coming I'm Coming', 'Stranger Blues' [live], 'Coming Your Way' [live], 'Rattlesnake Shake' [live]

INCLUDES LIVE TRACKS FROM BOSTON AND LONDON, FOUR TRACKS BY THE Brunning Sunflower Blues Band, one track by Green with Nick Pickett and five with Green and Duster Bennett. There's an interesting fold-out illustrated cover with text. The early version of 'Man Of The World' is remarkably fragile when it starts but has a great drum sound in the louder bridge. The take was presumably rejected owing to slight mis-timing on some of the guitar phrases. Another notable track is 'Blues In B♭ minor', an instrumental take of 'Before The Beginning'.

Fleetwood Mac

[The Best Of The Best Gold CD Series]

Sony International 2002

TRACKS: 'Need Your Love So Bad', 'Coming Home', 'Rambling Pony', 'Big Boat' [Eddie Boyd], 'I Believe My Time Ain't Long', 'Sun Is Shing', 'Albatross', 'Black Magic Woman', 'Just The Blues' [Eddie Boyd], 'Jigsaw Puzzle Blues', 'Looking For Somebody', 'Stop Messin' Round', 'Shake Your Money Maker', 'Love That Burns'

THIS IS A NEW PRESSING OF A 1989 IMPORT COMPILATION FROM SONY Germany with a different track-listing from the 1971 *Greatest Hits*.

Madison Blues

Shakedown Records ShakeBX110z (2003)

CD 1 [STUDIO]: 'Hey Baby', 'It's You I Miss', 'Gone Into The Sun', 'Tell Me You Need Me', '[studio', 'live] Crazy About You (Can't Hold Out Much Longer)', 'Down At The Crown', 'Tell Me All The Things You Do', 'Station Man', 'Purple Dancer' [live in concert], 'Station Man', 'Crazy About You', 'One Together', 'I Can't Stop Loving Her', 'Lonely Without You', 'Tell Me All The Things You Do', 'Jewel-Eyed Lady'

CD 2 [LIVE IN CONCERT]: 'Madison Blues', 'Purple Dancer', 'Open The Door', 'Preaching Blues', 'Dust My Broom', 'Get Like You Used To', 'Don't Go Please Stay', 'Station Man', 'I'm On My Way', 'Jailhouse Rock', 'The King Speaks' [narrative], 'Teenage Darlin'', 'Honey Hush

CD 3: 96 min DVD interview with Jeremy Spencer filmed February 19, 2002

The Best Of Peter Green's Fleetwood Mac

Columbia 5101552 (2002)

TRACKS: 'Albatross', 'Black Magic Woman', 'Need Your Love So Bad' (US version), 'My Heart Beat Like A Hammer', 'Rollin' Man', 'The Green Manalishi (With The Two-Pronged Crown)', 'Man Of The World', 'Something Inside Of Me', 'Looking For Somebody', 'Oh Well Part 1', 'Oh Well Part 2', 'Rattlesnake Shake', 'Merry Go Round', 'I Loved Another Woman', 'Need Your Love Tonight', 'Worried Dream', 'Dragonfly', 'Stop Messin' Around', 'Shake Your Moneymaker', 'I'd Rather Go Blind' [Chicken Shack], 'Albatross' [Chris Coco feat. Peter Green]

THIS 20-TRACK SINGLE CD EFFECTIVELY ECLIPSES THE 1971 *GREATEST HITS*. All but one ('Love That Burns') of that album's tracks are present, to which are added a number of other cuts. The Chicken Shack track is included because Christine McVie has the lead vocal. There is a new recording/update of 'Albatross' by Chris Coco with Peter Green 'featured'. This is done in a high-tech ambient style and is not as dire as either the idea or the dread word 'featuring' might lead you to anticipate. Green's guitar is quite a way back in the mix and doesn't possess anything like the strength or tone of the original.

The Very Best Of Fleetwood Mac

Warner Bros 812273635 2 (2002)

UK VERSION: 'Go Your Own Way', 'Don't Stop', 'Dreams', 'Little Lies', 'Everywhere', 'Albatross', 'You Make Loving Fun', 'Rhiannon' [single version], 'Black Magic Woman', 'Tusk', 'Say You Love Me', 'Man Of The World', 'Seven Wonders', 'Family Man', 'Sara', 'Monday Morning', 'Gypsy', 'Over My Head' [single version], 'Landslide', 'The Chain', 'Big Love' [live 1997]

US VERSION: CD1: 'Monday Morning', 'Dreams', 'You Make Loving Fun', 'Go Your Own Way', ' Rhiannon', 'Say You Love Me', 'I'm So Afraid', 'Silver Springs', 'Over My Head', 'Never Going Back Again', Sara', ' Love In Store', 'Tusk',

'Landslide', 'Songbird', 'Big Love' CD2: 'The Chain', 'Don't Stop', 'What Makes You Think You're The One', 'Gypsy', 'Second Hand News', 'Little Lies', 'Think about Me', 'Go Insane' [live 1997], 'Gold Dust Woman', 'Hold Me', 'Seven Wonders', 'World Turning', 'Everywhere', 'Sisters Of The Moon', 'Family Man', 'As Long As You Follow', 'No Questions Asked', 'Sky's The Limit', 'Paper Doll'

A 21-TRACK COMPILATION THAT THROWS IN THREE SONGS FROM THE PETER Green era with the US-model Mac. Five tracks from the 1975 *Fleetwood Mac* album and *Rumours*, four from *Tango In The Night*, two from *Tusk*, one from *Mirage* and one from *The Dance*. In the US it was expanded to two CDs and 36 tracks; the three Peter Green-era tracks were dropped and instead you get almost all of *Rumours*. The US CD is enhanced with footage of the band making the *Say You Will* album and other treats.

MISCELLANEOUS
Simply The Best

Connoisseur Collection 1996

TRACKS: 'Respectable' [Cheynes], 'If You Wanna Be Happy' [Peter B's Looners], 'Double Trouble' [John Mayall], 'Fleetwood Mac' [Fleetwood Mac], 'I'd Rather Go Blind' [Chicken Shack], 'Shape I'm In' [Jeremy Spencer], 'When You Say' [Christine Perfect], 'Put A Record On' [Tramp], 'Ram Jam City' [Danny Kirwan], 'Sentimental Lady' [Bob Welch], 'We Just Disagree' [Dave Mason], 'Gold' [John Stewart], 'Don't Say No' [Billy Burnette], 'Rattlesnake Shake' [Mick Fleetwood], 'Stop Draggin' My Heart Around' [Stevie Nicks, Tom Petty], 'Now I Know' [John McVie]

A MISCELLANY OF TRACKS FROM BAND MEMBERS ACROSS THE MAC'S career, before, during or after they were in the band.

If you fancy hearing what Fleetwood Mac's music sounds like in other people's hands there are a number of options. *Legacy: A Tribute to Fleetwood Mac's Rumours* (Atlantic 1998) features some big names like Elton John, The Corrs, Matchbox 20, The Cranberries, and Jewel doing the entire LP. For a more left-field interpretation by various artists there is *Fleetwood Mac: Patron Saints Of Pop* (Undercover 1997). Nic Johnston recorded an album of acoustic guitar arrangements (Chicago 1997). For the 'classical' taste try Gary Tesca Orchestra (Mirage Instrumental 1996), the London Rock

Orchestra (and guests) (Cass Records 1996), *The String Quartet Tribute to Fleetwood Mac* (Vitamin Records 2003), or the LPO (Platinum Discis 2001). Beyond this lies only karaoke... There are a few interview discs on the market, such as the one on Baktabak Records (1995) – approach with extreme caution. To hear some of the blues originals on which the Peter Green-era band based their repertoire try *The Blues Roots of Fleetwood Mac* (Catfish Records 2000).

VIDEO

Peter Green's Fleetwood Mac: The Early Years 1967-70

PNE Video PNV1008; Released 1994

TRACKS: 'Black Magic Woman', 'Heart Beat Like A Hammer', 'Shake Your Moneymaker', 'I'm Worried', 'Like It This Way', 'World Keep On Turning', 'Stop Messing Around', 'Albatross', 'Need Your Love So Bad', 'Man Of The World', 'Like Crying', 'Linda', 'Oh Well', 'Rattlesnake Shake', 'Green Manalishi' (55 mins).

THIS IS A COMPILATION OF LIVE TELEVISION PERFORMANCES, STILLS ETC. IT'S interesting in parts but frustrating overall because of the poor quality of most of the material. This is now available as a DVD (Image Entertainment 1999).

Fleetwood Mac
Documentary
And Live Concert

US And UK Warner Home Video, Wea PEV 4022; Released 1981

TRACKS: 'Sisters Of The Moon', 'Walk A Thin Line', 'Angel', 'Save Me A Place', 'Tusk', 'Songbird', 'The Chain', 'Go Your Own Way', 'Never Make Me Cry', 'Sara', 'Think About Me', 'Not That Funny'

In Concert Mirage Tour
1982

US RCA Columbia Pictures Home Video 1984; UK RCA RVT 10134

TRACKS: 'The Chain', 'Gypsy', 'Love In Store', 'Not That Funny', 'You Make Loving Fun', 'I'm So Afraid', 'Blue Letter', 'Rhiannon', 'Tusk', 'Eyes Of The World', 'Go Your Own Way', 'Sisters Of The Moon', 'Songbird'

RE-ISSUED AS *FLEETWOOD MAC IN CONCERT* ON CHANNEL FIVE VIDEO CFV 00032, March 1986. Footage of the Mirage tour. There appears to be a Brazilian DVD of this concert which has not been released in the US.

Tango In The Night

Warner Reprise Video 938149-3; September 1988

TRACKS: 'The Chain', 'Everywhere', 'Dreams', 'Seven Wonders', 'Isn't It Midnight', 'World Turning', 'Little Lies', 'Oh Well', 'Gold Dust Woman', 'Another Woman', 'Stand Back', 'Songbird', 'Don't Stop' (60 mins)

THIS WAS FILMED AT THE COW PALACE, SAN FRANCISCO DECEMBER 12 & 13, 1987, with the six-piece line-up with Asante on percussion. Nicks alone had 'additional photography' several months later - i.e. she re-filmed all her close-ups. This is now available as a Region 1 DVD (WEA 2003).

Fleetwood Mac:
Video Biography

MCEG Virgin Vision VVD 268; 1988

A DOCUMENTARY.

The Dance

Warner Bros Video 7599 38386-3 (1997) 106 Mins

TRACKS: 'The Chain', 'Dreams', 'Everywhere', 'Gold Dust Woman', 'I'm So Afraid', 'Temporary One', 'Bleed To Love Her', 'Gypsy', 'Big Love', 'Go Insane', 'Landslide', 'Say You Love Me', 'You Make Loving Fun', 'My Little Demon', 'Silver Springs', 'Over My Head', 'Rhiannon', 'Sweet Girl', 'Go Your Own Way', 'Tusk', 'Don't Stop', 'Songbird

THE VIDEO OF THE NEW ALBUM OF OLD FAVOURITES GARNISHED WITH A few newies, filmed in Burbank, California, in May 1997, before an ecstatic audience of Mac-o-philes. Note that 'Gold Dust Woman', 'Gypsy', 'Go Insane', 'Over My Head' and 'Songbird' are not on the CD of *The Dance*, and the track order has some changes, with 'Rhiannon' moving much later in the set. A happy time guaranteed for all. This is now available as a Region 1 DVD.

Index